MORE

SNO

sites in Wes

DEPARTMENT OF CONSERVATION AND LAND MANAGEMENT

CONTENTS

Foreword

Our first book in this series, *Dive and Snorkel Sites in Western Australia,* has been widely acclaimed by both divers and snorkellers, and the diving industry. This excellent field guide sold out within two years and is now in its second print run. It also won the Media Category of the 1997 Western Australian Tourism Awards, in recognition of its contribution to the development and promotion of diving tourism.

However, since publishing *Dive and Snorkel Sites in Western Australia,* CALM has been approached by many people wishing to tell us about magnificent dive sites that were not included in the first book. CALM has also been involved in the development of an important marine park proposed at Jurien Bay. Thus *More Dive and Snorkel Sites in Western Australia* features dives around Esperance, Albany, Mandurah, Jurien and the Dampier Archipelago, regions which were not included in the first book, but which offer diving comparable to that found in existing marine parks. We have also revisited Marmion Marine Park, Shoalwater Islands Marine Park, Rottnest Island Marine Reserve, Shark Bay Marine Park and Ningaloo Marine Park, but with entirely new sites.

Whether you are a snorkeller, a novice SCUBA diver or a diver with considerable experience, we are sure you will enjoy them.

Dr Syd Shea
EXECUTIVE DIRECTOR
Department of Conservation and Land Management

Introduction

ABOUT THIS BOOK

More Dive and Snorkel Sites in Western Australia is designed primarily for snorkellers and novice divers. Almost all of the sites are in depths of 18 metres or less. Four sites are deeper than 18 metres and these should only be attempted if the diver is qualified to dive below 18 metres. There is a strong emphasis on shore dives and dives within marine parks. However, there are also many boat dives that experienced divers would find challenging and enjoyable, and some moderately difficult shore dives.

It is difficult to grade these dives because many dives that seemed "easy" might be difficult in certain weather conditions. Read the information provided about the skill required and caution areas carefully and assess the weather before attempting any dive, even those graded easy. It would be possible to encounter difficulties in almost all of the sites in adverse weather or strong currents. Even a little swell can affect visibility, so it may be better to wait for optimum conditions.

The mud maps are intended to be used as a rough guide only, and are not drawn to scale. Scales and distances given are only approximate. Please do not place too much emphasis on their accuracy, and balance the information provided here with your own judgement. Always keep an eye open for potential hazards that may not have been evident when the sites were mapped, and match the dive sites with your level of skill. Your safety is our concern but your responsibility.

CARING FOR THE MARINE ENVIRONMENT

Coral reefs, eerie shipwrecks, caves, limestone harbour walls, tropical lagoons and forests of kelp are just some of the diverse features of Western Australia's underwater world. Each place has its own array of natural wonders. Marmion Marine Park, for example, is home to Australian sea lions. The park's eroded limestone reefs are a diver's paradise, forming ledges, caverns and swimthroughs. They are inhabited by a wonderful array of temperate and tropical fish species and colourful invertebrates. To the north, Ningaloo Marine Park offers a vastly different diving experience. It protects a 260-kilometre-long reef, that is partly a fringing reef and partly a barrier reef. This is one of only two large coral reef systems to occur on the western edge of a continent. It is also the only large reef found so close to a continental land mass; about 100 metres offshore at its closest point.

Diving in marine reserves

Several important and representative underwater habitats are protected in marine reserves (which include all marine parks) managed by the Department of Conservation and Land Management (CALM). There are marine parks at Marmion, Shoalwater Islands (near Rockingham), Shark Bay and Ningaloo (near Exmouth). A number of other areas have been proposed for consideration as marine reserves, and these waters may be declared as such at some stage in the future. These include the proposed marine park offshore from Jurien Bay. This reef system is the longest temperate barrier reef system in Australia (slightly longer than Ningaloo Reef). Being in a major zone of biogeographic overlap, it also supports a very interesting and diverse mixture of tropical and temperate marine plants and animals, including stunning corals.

The purpose of marine reserves is to ensure that their underwater habitat and ecosystems are conserved indefinitely. WA's marine parks are zoned to ensure that users of the park don't impinge on each other's activities. There are three different zone categories.

Sanctuary zones are areas where visitors may "look but not touch". No fishing of any kind is permitted in these areas and all marine plants and animals are totally protected. They serve as benchmark areas to monitor any changes in adjacent areas in which fishing is allowed, and as replenishment zones, which allow new fish to repopulate nearby depleted reef communities in the event of excessive use. They also enable visitors to experience pristine coral and reef communities.

Recreation zones exclude commercial activities, but generally permit recreational activities such as fishing, provided that fishing regulations are followed. It is the diver's responsibility to ensure that he or she is up-to-date with current regulations and bag limits, holds any applicable licenses and only takes marine animals such as rock lobsters or abalones during the declared seasons. Regulations may vary from park to park. *General use zones* provide for commercial fishing and other uses that are consistent with conservation. In some cases, *special purpose zones* may be declared to meet the conservation needs of a particular area, if the three zone framework does not fit the situation.

There are also many other beautiful and ecologically significant areas outside marine parks that are heavily used by divers, but which are not at present subject to any management control. It is up to the individual diver to ensure that his or her activities maintain the environment in its natural state.

Other protected areas

Wrecks are protected under an Act, administered by the WA Maritime Museum, which prohibits the removal of artefacts or wilful damage of any sort. Please help to preserve our maritime heritage by leaving wrecks undisturbed.

The waters around Rottnest Island are protected by a marine reserve managed by the Rottnest Island Authority, and no spearfishing is allowed within these waters. Within the reserve, fishing is completely banned in some areas, such as the Kingston Reefs out from Thomson Bay.

Maintaining the underwater environment

Diving can affect unspoilt marine communities in many ways. Activities such as spearfishing, harvesting or collecting marine life may disrupt normal marine communities, by altering the number and diversity of species. Divers can easily select the site and type of fish they wish to take, a practice which can result in exploitation of certain species at particular sites, upsetting the natural balance.

While the impact of one diver may be minimal, many dive sites are visited by thousands. Because it is so easy to reach from Hillarys Boat Harbour, Boyinaboat Reef, a limestone outcrop in the Marmion Marine Park off metropolitan Perth, is visited by up to 100 divers a day during peak summer periods.

Marine manners

Interaction with aquatic plants and animals is both a privilege and a responsibility. When you dive, make up your mind to leave an area as it was before you arrived, avoiding undue disturbance to the marine environment and its resident plants and animals. Leave marine invertebrates where you find them, for all to enjoy, and if you pick up a rock or a shell always put it back where you found it. Virtually anything you pick up will probably have an animal living in it.

Make sure your diving gear is secured and not dangling, and watch where you're kicking: fins can break off coral and other invertebrate life, and so does touching with your hands. Good buoyancy control is important so that you don't crash into animals such as corals. You should also take great care when settling on the bottom; quiet, smooth movement is less likely to disturb animals and will let you observe aquatic life behaving naturally, rather than fleeing or hiding.

Follow these simple guidelines and you will be sure to enjoy some wonderful diving!

DIVING SAFELY

SCUBA diving and snorkelling have claimed lives, and divers should never become complacent about safe diving practices.

Never dive on SCUBA if you have not completed an accredited course. Many of the sites mapped and described in this book can be explored by snorkelling. You do not have to be a qualified SCUBA diver to learn about and enjoy the marine environment. However, it is recommended that you complete an accredited snorkelling training program.

Prior to diving, ensure you are using the correct equipment for the conditions, particularly if you haven't dived in the area before or if you haven't dived on SCUBA for awhile. Check all of your equipment thoroughly to ensure it is in good working order, and ensure you have the correct number of weights and a suitable exposure suit for the conditions. A compass and knife are standard safety equipment. Always carry essential spare parts such as mask and fin straps, O-rings and a first aid kit. Ensuring you have the right equipment on the day will make your dive safer and much more enjoyable.

Always check the weather forecast on the morning of your dive. However, don't just rely on the forecast, and assess the dive site thoroughly before entering the water. If you are uncertain about the suitability of the weather conditions for your planned dive, ask at the local dive shop. They will probably be able to suggest an alternative site if conditions are unsuitable. Be flexible and alter your plans if necessary.

Regardless of whether you are snorkelling or SCUBA diving, always display a dive flag and always dive with a buddy. If diving from a vessel, make sure someone is left to watch the boat (refer to the Safe Boating section on page 12). Before diving, you and your buddy should:

1. Inform a friend where you are diving and your estimated time of return;
2. Establish entry and exit points and techniques;
3. Choose a course to follow, taking currents and other factors into consideration;
4. After consulting dive tables, agree on a maximum time and depth limit;
5. Establish and review communication procedures and revise hand signals;
6. Agree on an air pressure for returning to the surface, usually 50 bar;
7. Decide what to do if separated; and
8. Discuss what to do should an emergency arise.

Before entering the water, ensure you and your buddy run through the five point equipment check:

1. BCD – needs to be snugly adjusted and operating properly. It should be partially inflated before you enter the water;
2. Weight belt – should be fitted with weight savers, have a right hand release and be free of all equipment and straps;
3. Releases – check to see where they are and ensure they are all secure;
4. Air – check that your buddy's air is turned on, ensure that the regulators are working, note where the alternate air source is and how it is used and make sure the air pressure hoses are not tangled;
5. Final – make a final once over for dangling straps and missing equipment.

Always use an approved dive table and stay within its limits. While diving, keep track of the time, depth, direction, temperature and air supply at all times. And don't forget that at the end of your dive you should ascend slowly and cautiously. A five minute safety stop at five metres is recommended. While ascending, keep an eye out for any boats in the area.

In the event of decompression sickness or any other diving accident call Fremantle Hospital at Alma Street in Fremantle, which coordinates the treatment of all cases of civilian diving accidents. Call (08) 9431 3333 and immediately state that the call is about a diving related accident. To report a boating accident, or to initiate a search, call Police Communications on (08) 9222 1111.

SAFE BOATING

The ocean deserves your greatest respect at all times. Even experienced boaters can occasionally find themselves in serious difficulties. However, if you plan your trip well and take care to observe standard safety precautions, you will minimise the chances of any problems occurring.

Always check the weather forecast before you leave and take it into account in deciding where you should go, the load you can safely carry and the people you take with you. Remember that a sea of 1.5 metres is about the maximum for comfort on a trailable-sized boat. This is the approximate wave height that a steady wind of about 15 knots will build up. A swell of 1.5 metres on a calm sea can also preclude diving. Cancel the trip if necessary. Keep an eye on the weather at all times while you are on the water, and head for shore if you see a thunderstorm developing. You should also consider accompanying another boat – operating in pairs will increase your safety.

Always carry the minimum safety equipment on board, including:

- a bilge pump (mandatory on boats at least seven metres long, unless they have sealed, self-draining decks), bailer or bucket;
- a suitable fire extinguisher;
- suitable life jackets for each person on board;
- an effective anchor and line;
- two parachute distress flares, approved to Australian Safety Standards;
- two hand-held orange smoke signals or one smoke canister;
- a two-way marine band radio; and
- an emergency positioning indicator radio beacon (EPIRB).

Although a Global Positioning System (GPS) is not mandatory, these systems are a good investment, and will help you to relocate good dive sites and maintain a constant watch on your location. It is recommended that you check with the Department of Transport for current information on the minimum safety equipment to meet legal standards.

To ensure you have a trouble-free and enjoyable trip, check that your boat, motor, fuel system and equipment are in good working order and ensure you are carrying enough fuel. Aim to have at least 25 per cent of your fuel left over, after completing your trip in the worst conditions you can imagine. In addition, make sure you have the correct charts, a compass, water, food, extra clothing, adequate tools and spares, an extra line for the anchor, as well as sunscreen, hats and other sun protection.

Decide where you intend to go, your expected time of return, the amount of fuel you will carry and where you intend to launch. Let somebody, preferably the duty officer at the local sea rescue group, know about your excursion and provide them with the names and phone numbers of the people on board, a description of your boat and registration numbers, your car and trailer registration numbers and a list of your safety equipment. If you logged on by radio, don't forget to log off.

When anchoring, it is wise to put out at least three times as much anchor line and chain as the depth of water you are anchoring in. For example, in 10 metres of water, put out at least a 30 metre anchor line. When anchoring close to reefs, consider the effects of sudden wind and sea changes on the position of your vessel. Play it safe and anchor in such a way that your vessel will lie in safe water regardless of such changes. And, of course, be considerate and don't anchor in coral or seagrass areas.

If divers are operating from a vessel they must display a signal to warn other boaters. The dive flag should be at least 750 millimetres long by 600 millimetres wide. The flag signifies that all boats should keep at least 50 metres clear. If this is not possible, then the boat must proceed at the slowest possible speed that allows full control and maintain a lookout.

Never leave your boat unattended. If the anchor line should snap while you are diving below, you will be stranded in deep water (literally).

FURTHER INFORMATION

There are a number of excellent publications about Western Australia's marine environment and the plants and animals that live in them, that will help you get more out of your diving.

The first book in this series, *Dive and Snorkel Sites in Western Australia,* is a good starting point to obtain more information about dive sites. Two excellent pocket-sized field guides to popular marine areas are *Discovering Penguin Island and the Shoalwater Islands Marine Park* and *Discovering Shark Bay Marine Park and Monkey Mia*. A larger, full colour field guide recently published is *The Marine Life of Coral Bay and the Ningaloo Marine Park*. All of these books are published by CALM.

In CALM's Bush Book series, which are also pocket-sized, there are the *Beachcombers Guide to South-West Beaches*, *Whales and Dolphins of Western Australia* and *Hazardous Animals of North-Western Australia*.

The Western Australian Museum publishes two excellent field guides to help you identify various fish species. They are *Marine Fishes of Tropical Australia and South-East Asia* and *The Marine and Estuarine Fishes of South-Western Australia*.

For further details about historic shipwrecks, contact the Western Australian Maritime Museum, which also publishes a number of detailed guides to many wrecks.

COBBLERS AND CONESHELLS

Many marine animals use venom or toxins for catching prey or defending themselves. Some of these may cause mild stings or rashes if contact is made with human skin. Only a few species have venoms or toxins potent enough to cause serious harm to people, and these are not often encountered. However, it is best to be aware of any problems they can cause and avoid coming into contact with them.

Blue-ringed octopuses (see page 41) and some species of fish-eating coneshells are among the most dangerous. These creatures kill their prey with a potent toxin injected with their bite and, although such cases are very rare, they have killed people. Blue-ringed octopuses live in reef flats and in tidal pools and can be recognised by their brilliant blue rings when disturbed. Be cautious when handling dead shells and when exploring underwater crevices or caves. Coneshells (see page 47) are conical and cylindrical in shape. They bury themselves in sand by day, and emerge at night to search for small fish, snails or worms. You should avoid picking up live coneshells.

Certain fish, such as catfish (also known as cobblers) and stingrays, have venomous spines and can cause painful injuries. Use common sense around these creatures, as well as toadfish, pufferfish, boxfish and porcupine fish. Although they may appear to be slow-moving and docile, they are capable of inflicting serious bites if handled.

Stonefish are found around the top two-thirds of the Australian coast. They inhabit coastal reefs and shallow mudflats and usually lie partially buried on the sea floor. If people tread on this animal the sharp venomous spines can pierce their feet, causing severe pain and tissue damage. Always wear strong footwear (not thongs) when walking in shallows. Shoes will also provide protection from razor shells, which also inhabit the shallows of northern Australia.

Sea-snakes are also found in marine areas, and some species are extremely venomous. They are quite curious and may approach, but if you don't touch them they should leave you alone. Bristleworms (ringed or segmented worms up to 20 centimetres long) often lie under rocks or in corals. Their bites may cause injury. So can the bristles, if they penetrate the skin. Be wary if turning over rocks or corals.

Sharks are also common inhabitants of our coastal waters and some species are dangerous. As with other potentially dangerous fish, don't be tempted to touch them, as they may try to defend themselves by biting.

In tropical areas, such as Ningaloo Marine Park, fire coral is found on the sand around reefs and fireweed can be found growing on reefs. These marine animals can cause a burning sensation. Wearing gloves and protective suits will avoid stings from accidentally brushing against them.

If you are unlucky enough to be bitten or otherwise poisoned by a marine animal, keep the injured limb still and seek immediate medical attention. However, most marine animals should not pose a problem unless harassed or inadvertently touched or trodden upon. Fortunately, most injuries can be avoided by simple common sense and behaving cautiously around any animal you are unsure about.

ESPERANCE TO BREMER BAY

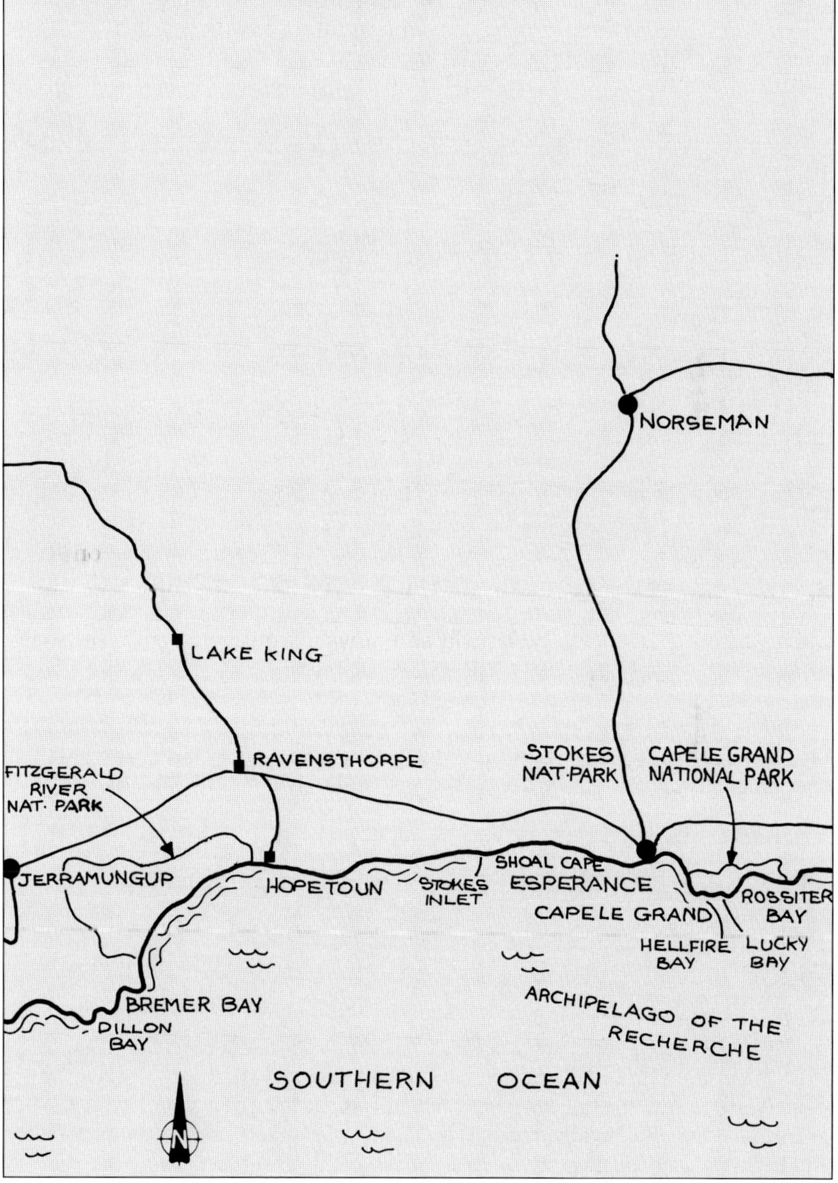

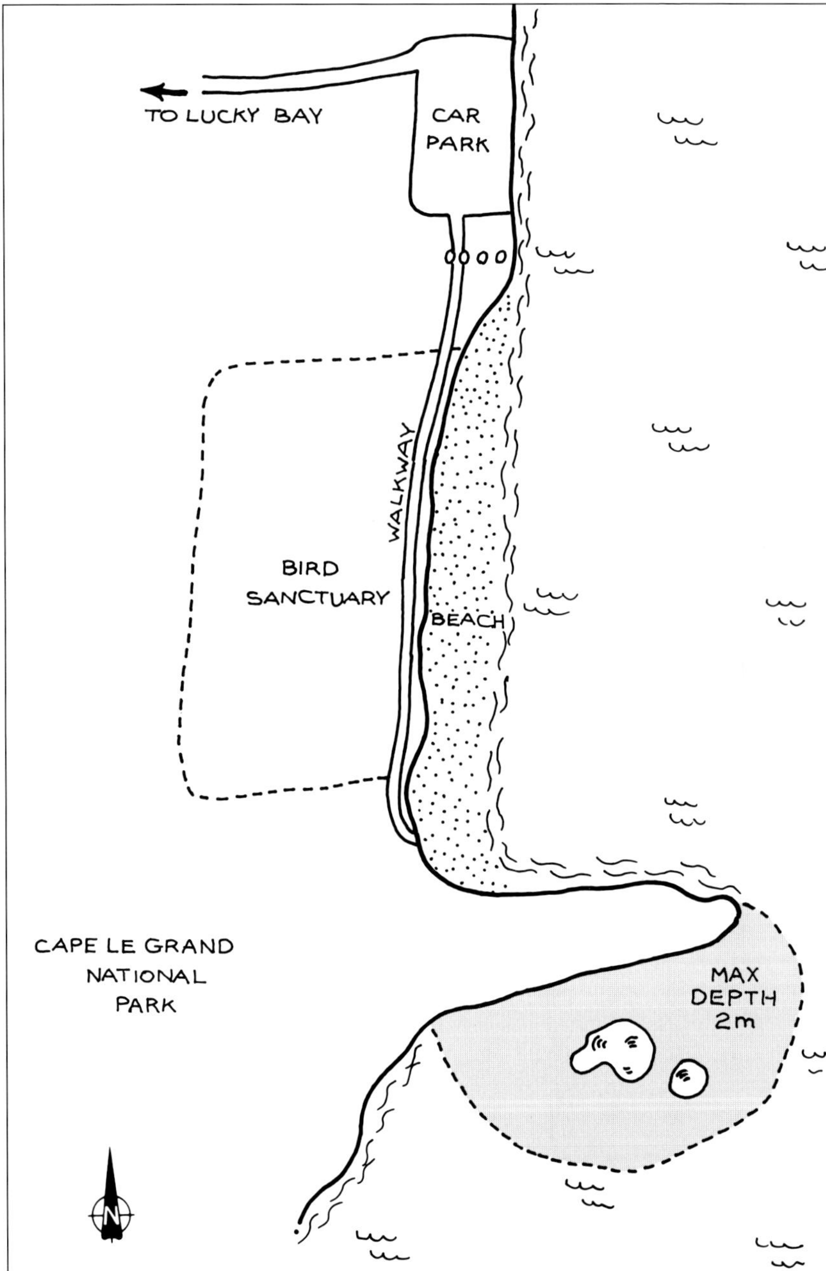
TO LUCKY BAY
CAR PARK
WALKWAY
BIRD SANCTUARY
BEACH
CAPE LE GRAND NATIONAL PARK
MAX DEPTH 2m

Rossiter Bay

1

How to get there: *By car, via Fisheries Road, Merivale Road and Cape Le Grand Road. The route is well signposted from Fisheries Road. The road from Lucky Bay to Rossiter Bay is gravel but this is no problem for 2WD vehicles.*
Depth: *Up to 12 metres.*

Rossiter Bay is in the Cape Le Grand National Park, some 57 kilometres from the Esperance townsite by road, or a much shorter distance via the beach from Wylie Bay to Cape Le Grand. This national park is one of Western Australia's best known and most spectacular, and Rossiter Bay is one of many picturesque bays along its coast. To reach the entry point of the dive, walk south from the car park, for about 200 metres. This walk will take you past the natural bird sanctuary. The area is dominated by large tall trees and these are the home of numerous species of birds. There are picnic tables and chairs nestled under the trees, so it is a great place to stop for a basket lunch and to enjoy nature at its best.

Over the headland, you will see two large rocks that emerge from the water. Around them is the dive site. It is an area of tumbled granite boulders with ledges, swimthroughs and lots of nooks and crannies to explore. This dive site is quite safe with no currents etc, and is ideal for beginners, who may like to snorkel in the shallower water along the headland. The maximum depth is 12 metres, so the site also provides a challenge for the more experienced. The area has some large bommies and there is a good variety of fish species to see and identify.

Some of these fish species may include small groper, sweep, western blue devils, a variety of wrasse, colourful harlequin fish, leatherjackets, swallowtail nannygai, herring, whiting, trevally, yellowtail and possibly a queen snapper moving through the area. You may even see some Roe's or green-lipped abalone on the rocks in the shallower water.

Degree of difficulty: *Easy to moderate.*
Area's status: *The area lies offshore from Cape Le Grand National Park.*

Lesley Hudson, with assistance from Esperance Diving and Fishing

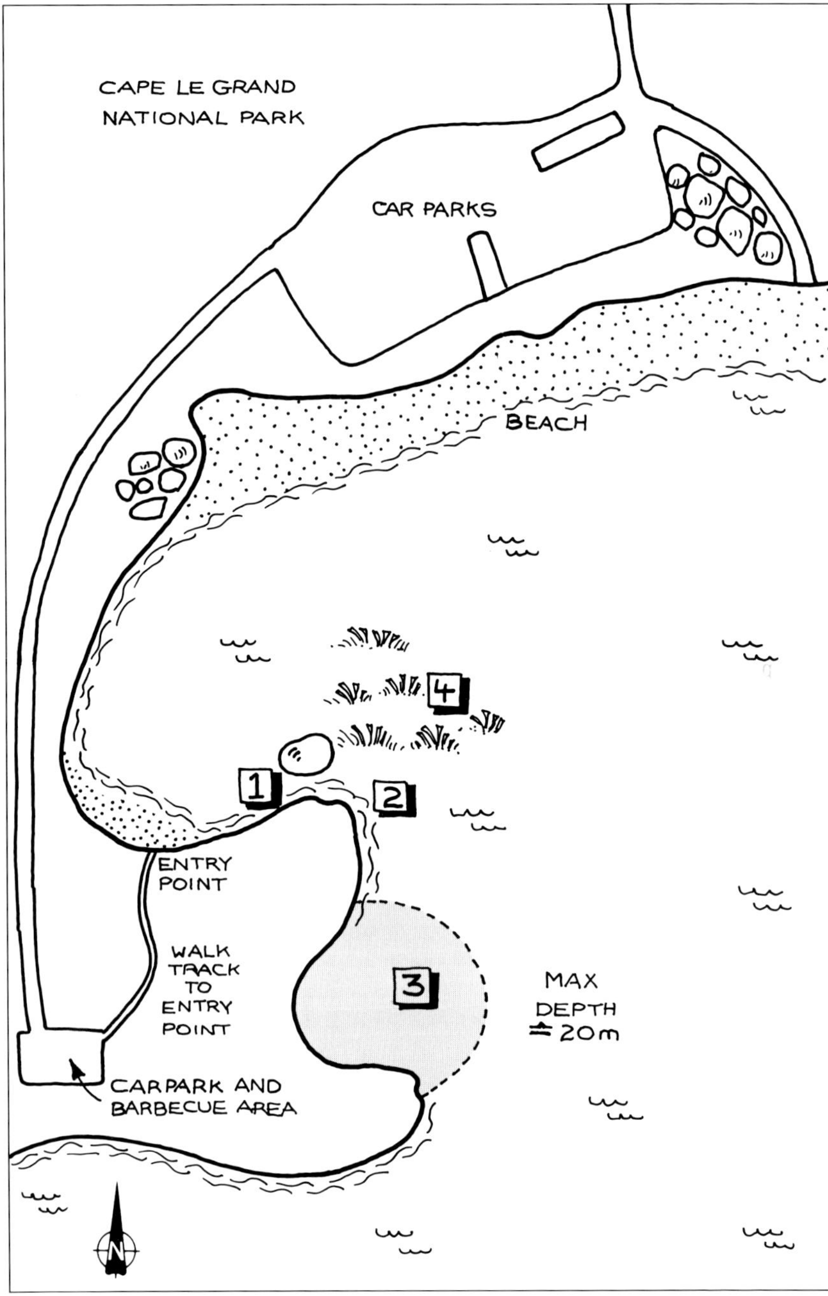

CAPE LE GRAND
NATIONAL PARK
CAR PARKS
BEACH
4
1
2
ENTRY
POINT
WALK
TRACK
TO
ENTRY
POINT
3
MAX
DEPTH
≏20m
CARPARK AND
BARBECUE AREA
N

Lucky Bay

How to get there: *By car from Esperance, via Fisheries Road, Merivale Road and Cape Le Grand Road. The route is well signposted from Fisheries Road and is accessible to 2WD vehicles.*
Depth: *3-22 metres.*

Lucky Bay is 57 kilometres from Esperance in the Cape Le Grand National Park. The bay has one of the most scenic beaches in the Esperance region, and provides a delightful snorkel and SCUBA dive in a very sheltered area. The site varies in depth from three to 22 metres, so is shallow enough for the novice snorkeller and provides depth for the more experienced. Facilities at Lucky Bay include barbecues, picnic areas, shade shelters, water and campsites (with septic toilets and showers).

1. Simply snorkel out to the right, heading around the granite headland.
2. Around the large rock, just out from the entry point, there are numerous submerged boulders. This shallow and very pretty area is well worthy of exploration.
3. Around the granite headland is an area that makes an excellent SCUBA dive, with a maximum depth of 22 metres. Fish species such as swallowtail, leatherjackets, wrasse, butterflyfish, western blue devils and sometimes schools of pilchards live in and around numerous submerged granite boulders. There is also a section of plate coral teeming with small fish. Caves, soft corals, sponges and plenty of invertebrate life add to the scenery.
4. If you look carefully in the seagrass (*Posidonia*) areas, you may be able to discern a leafy seadragon or be visited by a playful Australian sea lion. The sea lions breed and rest on several of the islands in the magnificent Archipelago of the Recherche, which stretches for more than 200 kilometres along the State's southern coast. Their fishing excursions can last for up to two days. Fish, squid, octopus, cuttlefish, small sharks and rock lobster form the basis of their varied diet. This species is the only seal or sea lion that is unique to Australian waters.

Caution areas: *Do not dive beyond your level of comfort or expertise.*
Degree of difficulty: *Easy to moderate.*
Area's status: *The area lies offshore from Cape Le Grand National Park.*

Lesley Hudson, with assistance from Esperance Diving and Fishing

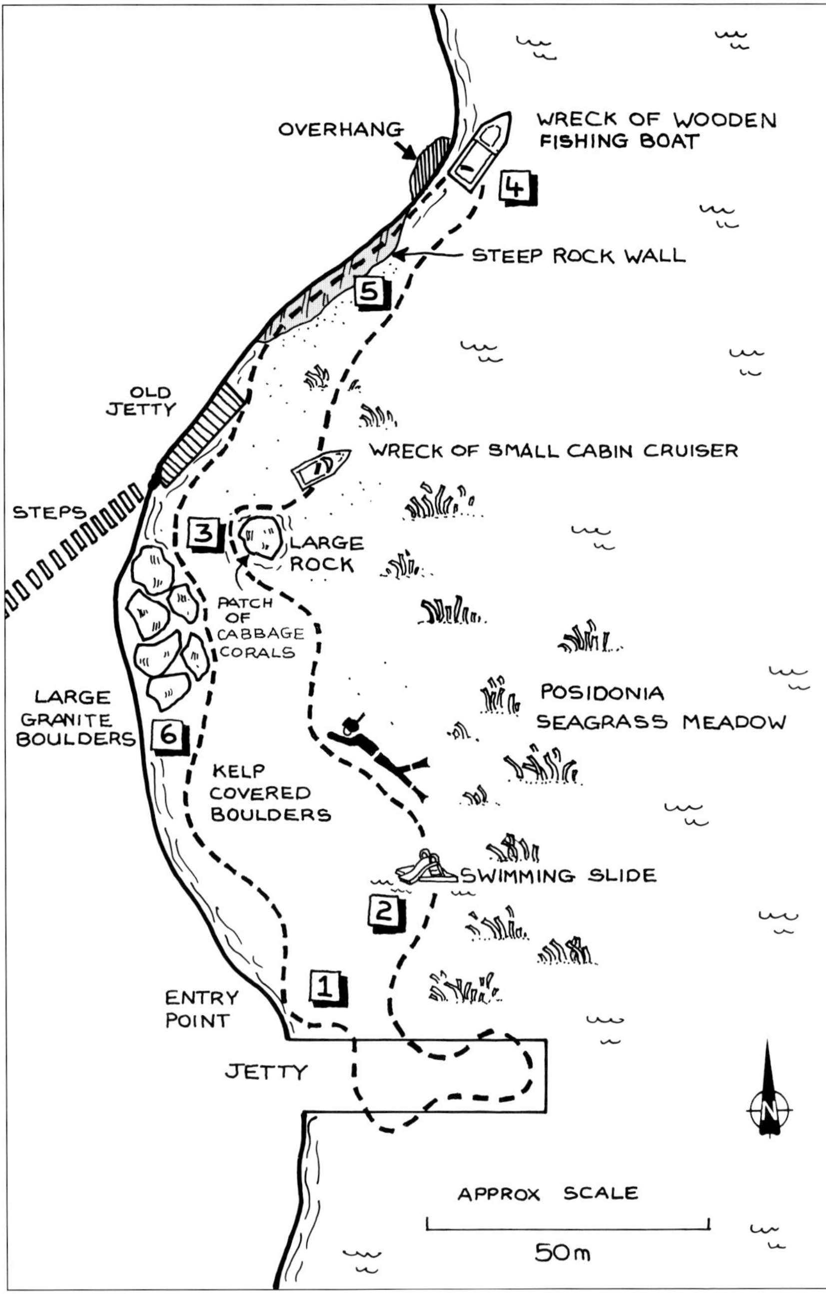
OVERHANG
WRECK OF WOODEN FISHING BOAT
4
STEEP ROCK WALL
5
OLD JETTY
WRECK OF SMALL CABIN CRUISER
STEPS
3
LARGE ROCK
PATCH OF CABBAGE CORALS
POSIDONIA SEAGRASS MEADOW
LARGE GRANITE BOULDERS
6
KELP COVERED BOULDERS
SWIMMING SLIDE
2
ENTRY POINT
1
JETTY
N
APPROX SCALE
50m

Woody Island

3

How to get there: *By ferry or other boat from Esperance.*
Depth: *Down to 8-10 metres.*

Woody Island is a nature reserve about 12 kilometres south-east of Esperance, towards Cape Le Grand National Park. Daily boat trips to the island are run by Mackenzie's Island Cruises. The area adjacent to the landing jetty, on the eastern side of the island, is an excellent dive and snorkel site. It is sheltered and easily accessible, has a variety of marine life, the wrecks of two small vessels and a number of other interesting features.

1. Enter the water either from the landing jetty or from the shore adjacent to the jetty. Swim around the pylons, which are encrusted with a colourful variety of seaweeds, gorgonian fan corals, soft corals, sea squirts and barnacles. Schools of bullseyes can often be seen sheltering beneath the jetty.
2. Swim across to the swimming slide, the legs of which are covered with a similar profusion of invertebrates and seaweed. A variety of fish can be seen amongst the kelp-covered boulders, including horseshoe leatherjackets, zebra fish and magpie perch. Slightly further out from the shore is an extensive seagrass (*Posidonia*) meadow.
3. Several isolated patches of cabbage coral (*Turbinaria* species) are visible as you swim across the granite boulders, including a large colony on the side of a huge rock that rises to within a few metres of the surface. Just north of this rock, in about five metres of water, is the wreck of a small cabin cruiser lying upright on the bottom. The cabin area is home to a number of dusky morwongs, moonlighters and schools of bullseyes.
4. Another wreck, this time of a small wooden fishing boat, can be found at the foot of a steep granite wall at a depth of eight to 12 metres. This wreck is relatively intact, and offers a number of interesting nooks and crannies to explore. There is a large overhang in the rock wall, located on the surface above the wreck, making it fairly easy to find.
5. The adjoining rock wall is covered with a myriad of seaweeds, sponges, sea squirts and soft corals, and it descends to a sand-covered sea bed at about 10 metres. The pylons of the old jetty are an interesting feature, but be wary of old fishing line, as it is a popular fishing spot.

6. Swim back towards the entry point, following the shoreline across large granite boulders and ledges. Check under these ledges and in crevices, where you may find some fish, particularly horseshoe leatherjackets and a number of delicate gorgonian fan corals.

Caution areas: *Watch out for vessels coming into the jetty and to the moorings north of the jetty. There may be some old fishing line wrapped around the pylons of both jetties, so be sure to carry a knife.*
Degree of difficulty: *Easy.*

Jeremy Colman

SPONGES

Sponges are found in large numbers, from mid-tide level near the shore down to the greatest depths of the ocean. The smallest are only a millimetre high when fully grown and the largest sponge known is about as big as a medium-sized barrel. Near the shore, sponges tend to encrust rocks and other structures. In shallow and deep seas, the forms vary from spherical, finger-shaped, bushy or tree-like, tubular, cup-shaped or funnel-shaped. Their texture varies from soft and readily compressible to as hard as stone.

Aristotle was the first to recognise, some 2000 years ago, that sponges were animals. In the sixteenth century, they were thought to be solidified sea foam, and in the seventeenth century it was suggested that they were the homes of marine worms. Otherwise the general impression was that sponges belonged to the plant kingdom.

The characteristic feature of a sponge is that it bears one or more conspicuous rounded openings. These are best described as vents. Under a microscope, the rest of the surface is seen to be punctured by minute pores.

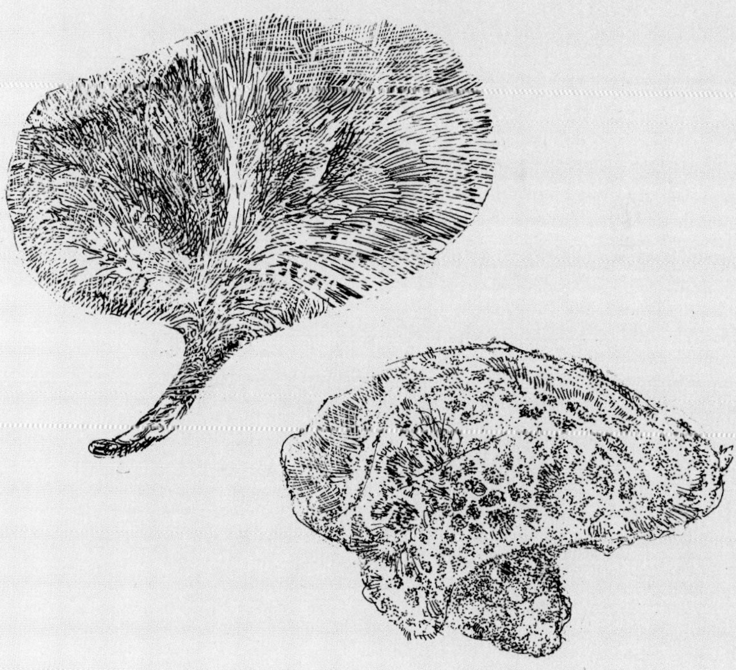

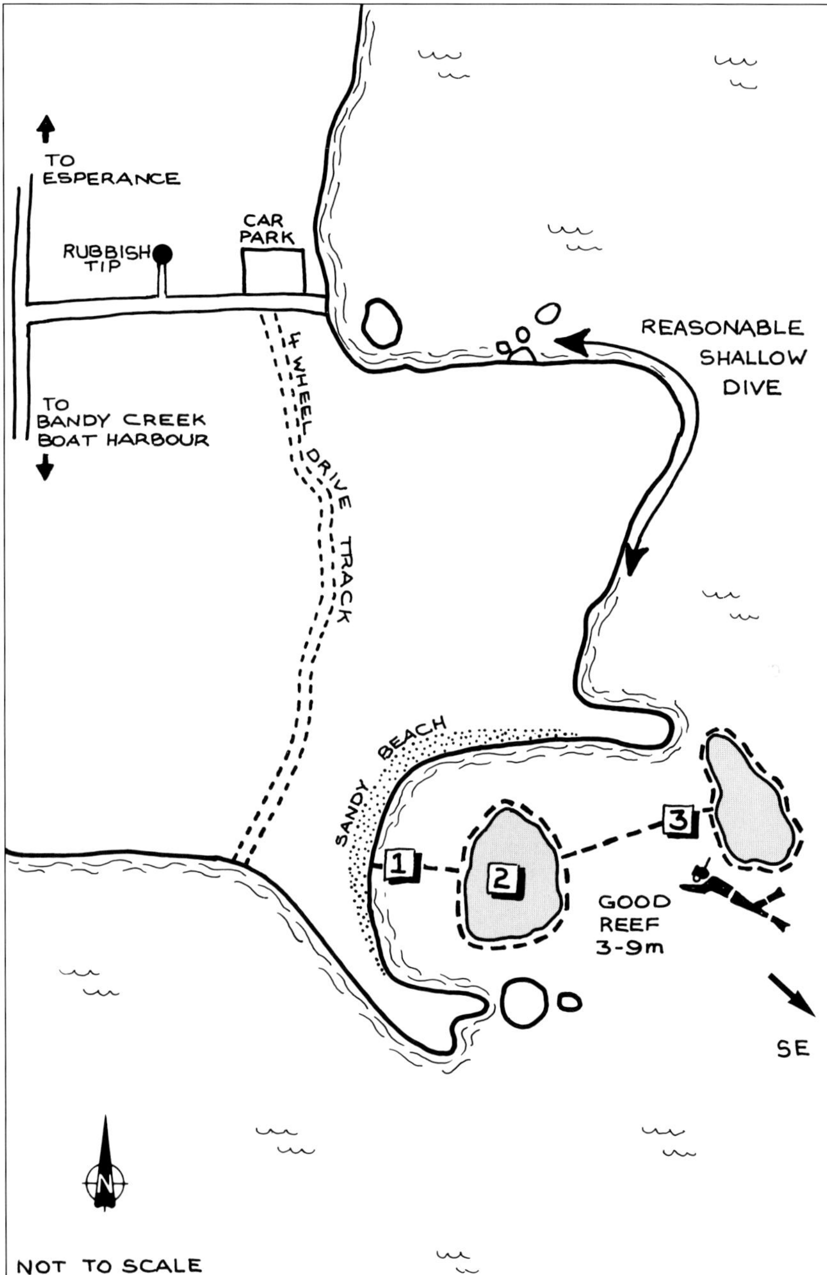
TO ESPERANCE
RUBBISH TIP
CAR PARK
TO BANDY CREEK BOAT HARBOUR
4 WHEEL DRIVE TRACK
REASONABLE SHALLOW DIVE
SANDY BEACH
1
2
3
GOOD REEF 3-9m
SE
N
NOT TO SCALE

Wylie Bay

4

How to get there: *By car, then swim from the shore.*
Depth: *3-9 metres.*

Wylie Bay is some 15 kilometres east of the Esperance townsite. You can either take the road out to Bandy Creek Boat Harbour (the professional fishing wharf) and drive via the beach to Wylie Bay or turn left about 500 metres before you get to the boat harbour, and drive via a sealed road to a car park at the end of the road. From the car park, you can walk over the sand dunes to the beach facing south. If you have a four-wheel-drive simply drive over the sand hills. This is also a great spot for a swim and a picnic as well as a snorkel dive. Avoid the site on a day when there is a swell, as the water will become surgy and the visibility will decline.

1. The beach faces two directions: south and south-east. Enter the water from the beach, facing south-east.
2. Directly out from the shore is a reef between three and nine metres deep. This consists largely of submerged granite boulders with some limestone. This is quite a complex area, with ledges, undercuts and undulating bottom. There is a variety of seaweeds and seagrasses, as well as sponges and soft corals.
3. Further out and off to the left is another submerged reef. To get to this, you pass over sand and seagrass. This is a slightly deeper reef with a good variety of fish to see and identify. Varieties that may be seen include queen snapper, groper, wrasse, leatherjackets, cod, western foxfish and sweep. Flatheads and stingrays may be seen on the sandy bottom, while abalones cling to the rocky bottom.
4. It is also quite a good snorkel if you continue left and swim right around to the other side of the headland. This area is only a few metres deep and is quite safe if you use the edge of the headland as your navigation guide.

Caution areas: *Avoid the site on a day when there is a swell.*
Degree of difficulty: *Easy to moderate, depending on conditions.*

Lesley Hudson, with assistance from Esperance Diving and Fishing

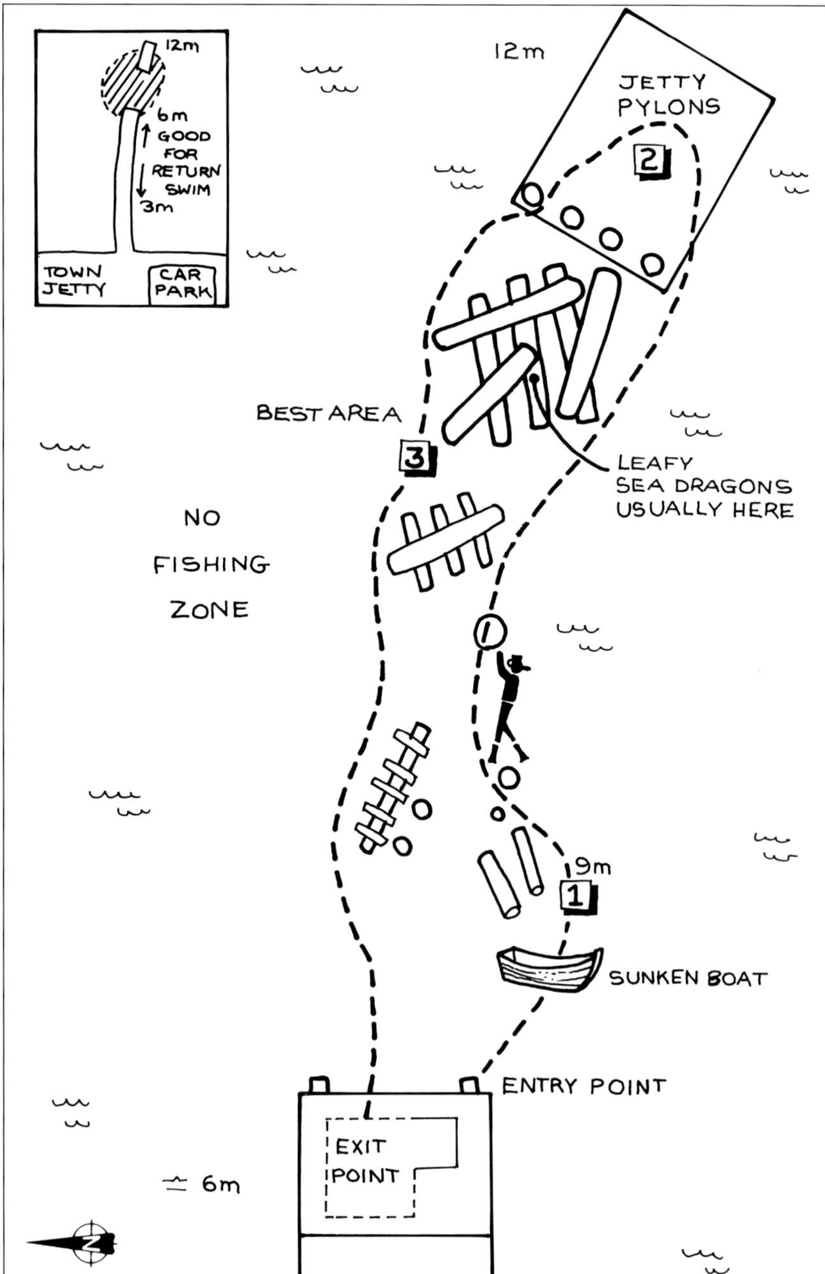
12m
6m
GOOD FOR RETURN SWIM
3m
TOWN JETTY
CAR PARK
12m
JETTY PYLONS
2
BEST AREA
3
LEAFY SEA DRAGONS USUALLY HERE
NO FISHING ZONE
9m
1
SUNKEN BOAT
ENTRY POINT
EXIT POINT
6m
N

Artificial Reef at Esperance Tanker Jetty 5

How to get there: *The jetty is near the Esperance town centre, along The Esplanade.*
Depth: *6-12 metres.*

The local dive club built this artificial reef from used tyres, which are strapped together in the shape of a pyramid. This reef was built between the end of the town jetty and the jetty island, which stands on its own some 150 metres from the end of the jetty. If you would like to do a SCUBA dive in this location, ask Esperance Diving and Fishing for a loan of their wheelbarrow. It will make the transport of your equipment to the end of the jetty, which is more than 600 metres long, a breeze.

1. Entry is from the eastern end of the Tanker Jetty, where a staircase takes you to a landing about 1.5 metres above the water. The jetty was once used by fuel tankers to unload their cargo. It is now extremely popular for fishing. One of the first points of interest is a small sunken boat in about nine metres of water.
2. The jetty island is swarming with fish and the pylons are prolific with colourful growth. Various types of nudibranchs (pronounced 'noo-dee-branks'), soft telesto corals and colourful sponges cling to the pylons. Australian sea lions are often seen in the vicinity of the jetty.
3. The tyres (many of which are no longer recognisable as such) and old, fallen jetty pylons have created habitat for marine life and a great variety of fish can be seen. Groper, queen snapper, swallowtail nannygai, western red snapper, large snook, dusky morwong, leatherjackets, herring, trevally and yellowtail are just a few of the species that inhabit the area. Magpie perch, easily recognised by the two wide dark bands on their bodies, are very common. Watch for majestic leafy seadragons. Leafy seadragons are well camouflaged, and look like a piece of drifting greenish-yellow seaweed. You will not see them anywhere else in the world, as they are unique to southern Western Australia and South Australia.

Caution areas: *Avoid diving or snorkelling the area if there is a swell.*
Degree of difficulty: *Easy to moderate, depending on conditions.*
Area's status: *The dive area (from about 20 metres from the end of the jetty to past the jetty island) is a 'no fishing zone', so divers are not able to spear fish and fishermen are not allowed to anchor over or fish on the reef.*

Lesley Hudson, with assistance from Esperance Diving and Fishing

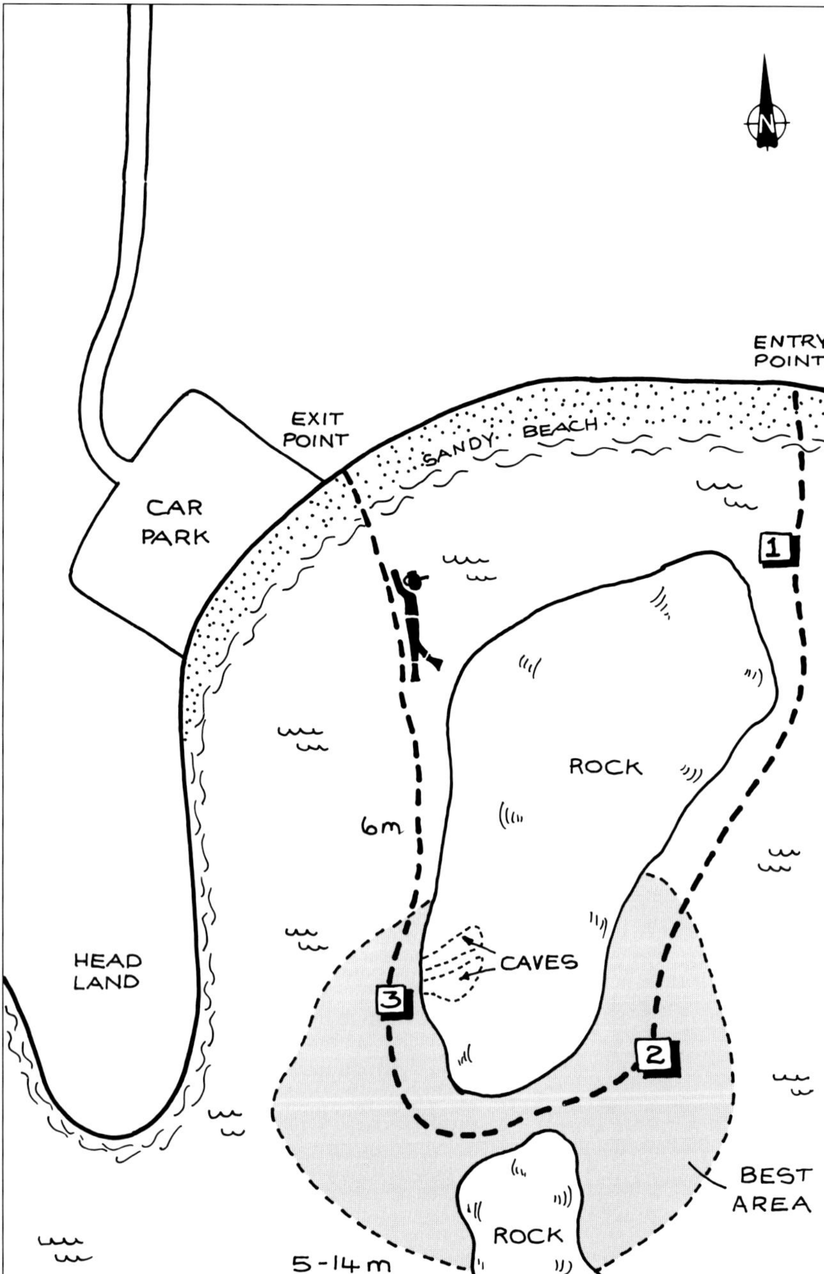
ENTRY POINT
EXIT POINT
SANDY BEACH
CAR PARK
ROCK
6m
CAVES
HEAD LAND
BEST AREA
ROCK
5-14m
1
2
3
N

Twilight Cove

6

How to get there: *By car from Esperance.*
Depth: *5-14 metres.*

Twilight Cove is off the Great Ocean Drive, about 10 kilometres from the town centre of Esperance. It is the most popular swimming beach close to Esperance, and also offers some great snorkelling and SCUBA diving. Divers need to be reasonable swimmers to attempt this, as it is quite a lengthy swim from the beach to the huge rocks that lie adjacent to the shore. Avoid diving the area if there is a swell, as the water movement between the large rocks and the shore will create a surge and the visibility will be reduced with increased sand movement.

1. It is best to start the dive by heading around the north-eastern side of the rocks. This area is only a metre or two deep and is basically sandy bottom.
2. The best part of the dive is behind the large rocks and in the gap between the rocks. This area increases in depth from 5 to 14 metres, and has tumbled boulders, rock crevices and ledges. There are lots of sponges and some colourful invertebrate life. Some of the fish species you could expect to see and identify are large inquisitive western blue groper, which grow to a length of 1.6 metres, sea sweep, queen snapper, herring, trevally, wrasse and sand whiting.
3. There are two very large caves, whose entrances lie on the western side of the large rock face. The cave entrances are small and well hidden by weed. The caves should not be entered by snorkellers. SCUBA divers would require a torch and would need to employ a responsible buddy system before entering. These caves are quite large and one of them goes back for several metres. The cave structures are lined with soft corals and sponges, so typical of the temperate waters surrounding Esperance, and are home to a large variety of smaller fish.

Caution areas: *Avoid diving or snorkelling the area if there is a south-westerly swell. Swimming into caves and under ledges can be hazardous.*
Degree of difficulty: *Moderate, depending on conditions.*

Lesley Hudson, with assistance from Esperance Diving and Fishing

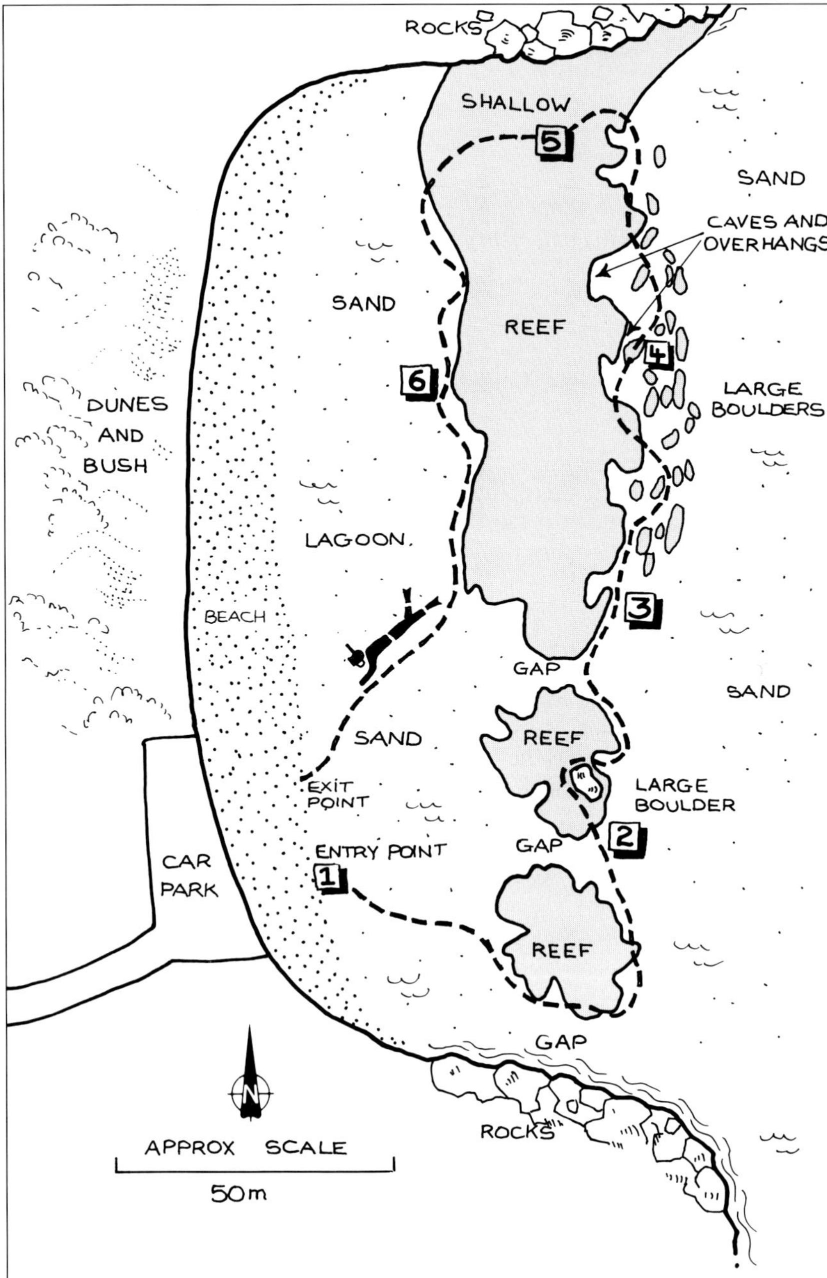
ROCKS
SHALLOW
5
SAND
CAVES AND
OVERHANGS
SAND
REEF
6
4
DUNES
AND
BUSH
LARGE
BOULDERS
LAGOON
BEACH
3
GAP
SAND
SAND
REEF
EXIT
POINT
LARGE
BOULDER
ENTRY POINT
GAP
2
CAR
PARK
1
REEF
GAP
N
ROCKS
APPROX SCALE
50m

Short Beach

7

How to get there: *Park at the Short Beach car park, about 6 km south of Bremer Bay, on the road out to Point Henry.*
Depth: *2-6 metres.*

This is a relatively sheltered location, with a white sandy beach and a lagoon protected by a line of reef about 25 metres from the shore. On calm days the inner edge of the reef is suitable for first time or novice snorkellers, and the more experienced can swim out through a number of gaps to snorkel or dive on the deeper seaward side of the reef. The visibility can be extremely good, and a wide range of fish species can usually be seen. Some of the vertical faces and overhanging ledges are covered in a colourful profusion of encrusting animals.

1. Enter the water right in front of the car park, and head out about 25 metres to the nearest area of reef at the southern end of the beach. As you swim across the lagoon, keep an eye open for rays that may be lying on the sand beneath you. Follow the edge of the first lump of reef around through the gap between the reef and the shore. Schools of silver drummer are common and will often follow divers and snorkellers as they swim along the reef.
2. As you swim north across the reef, you will cross an area of sand where there is a gap in the reef. A large boulder on the next area of reef has sheltered sides and ledges that are encrusted with gorgonian fan corals, soft corals, sea squirts and sponges. Numerous fish can be seen swimming over the kelp-covered boulders, or sheltering amongst the seaweeds, including scalyfins, zebra fish, herring cale, sea carp and red-lipped morwong.
3. Swimming north, you will cross another gap in the reef that leads into the lagoon. If you follow the outer reef edge you will reach an area where the reef drops off into slightly deeper water, with large boulders sticking out of the sandy bottom at a depth of about 6 metres. Other fish, including trevally, tommy rough, moonlighters, western king wrasse, banded sweep and sea sweep, can often be seen in this area. The reef also provides shelter for several larger species of fish, such as western blue groper and queen snapper.
4. Towards the northern end of the reef, there are a number of interesting caves and overhangs. Their walls are covered in a colourful variety of sponges, sea squirts, soft corals, and a bright red or orange gorgonian fan coral (*Mopsella* species). The caves and crevices are also home to schools of bullseyes and Woodward's pomfret,

a subtropical fish that is found on the South Coast as a result of the warming influence of the Leeuwin Current, and the dispersal of juvenile fish stages much further to the south and east of their normal ranges by this southward-flowing current.

5. The kelp cover shelters a number of smaller, more cryptically coloured fish, including brown-spotted wrasse, horseshoe leatherjackets and red-banded wrasse. The northern end of the reef runs into the rocks of the shoreline, but it is usually possible to turn inland and swim across the shallow reef top back into the lagoon. On very low tides it may be difficult to get across the reef at this point, and you may need to swim back along the reef to one of the gaps further south.
6. The sheltered side of the reef is fairly shallow and the seaweed covered boulders are home to large numbers of senator wrasse. You may also see blue-spotted goatfish lying on the sand close to the rocks. You can either swim directly to the beach, across the lagoon, or head along the inner edge of the reef and return to the beach just opposite the car park.

Caution areas: *The beach is exposed to easterly winds and swimming out through the gaps in the reef is difficult in any swell over half a metre. Swimming into caves and swimthroughs can be hazardous.*
Degree of difficulty: *Easy to moderate.*

Jeremy Colman

SEA ANEMONES

Sea anemones are carnivores that take an unusual guise. Their beautiful flower-like tentacles have a sinister purpose. Fish, snails or crabs that blunder into these waving fronds are soon paralysed by the stinging tentacles, engulfed by the central mouth and digested within the tube-like body. Anemones are usually brightly coloured, adopting shades of white, green, blue, orange, red or mauve.

These animals are generally fixed to reefs and other structures by the muscular disc at the base of the body. Though they usually move very little, they can creep along the bottom or may detach themselves and swim off. Anemones are closely related to jellyfish. The body is a tube-like column, which is divided internally into a number of partitions containing the digestive organs, muscles and gonads. Waste is excreted through the mouth, which is situated at the top of the body in the centre of the long tentacles. Some species of anemone also produce fully developed young through their mouths, which usually attach themselves to a rock near the parent.

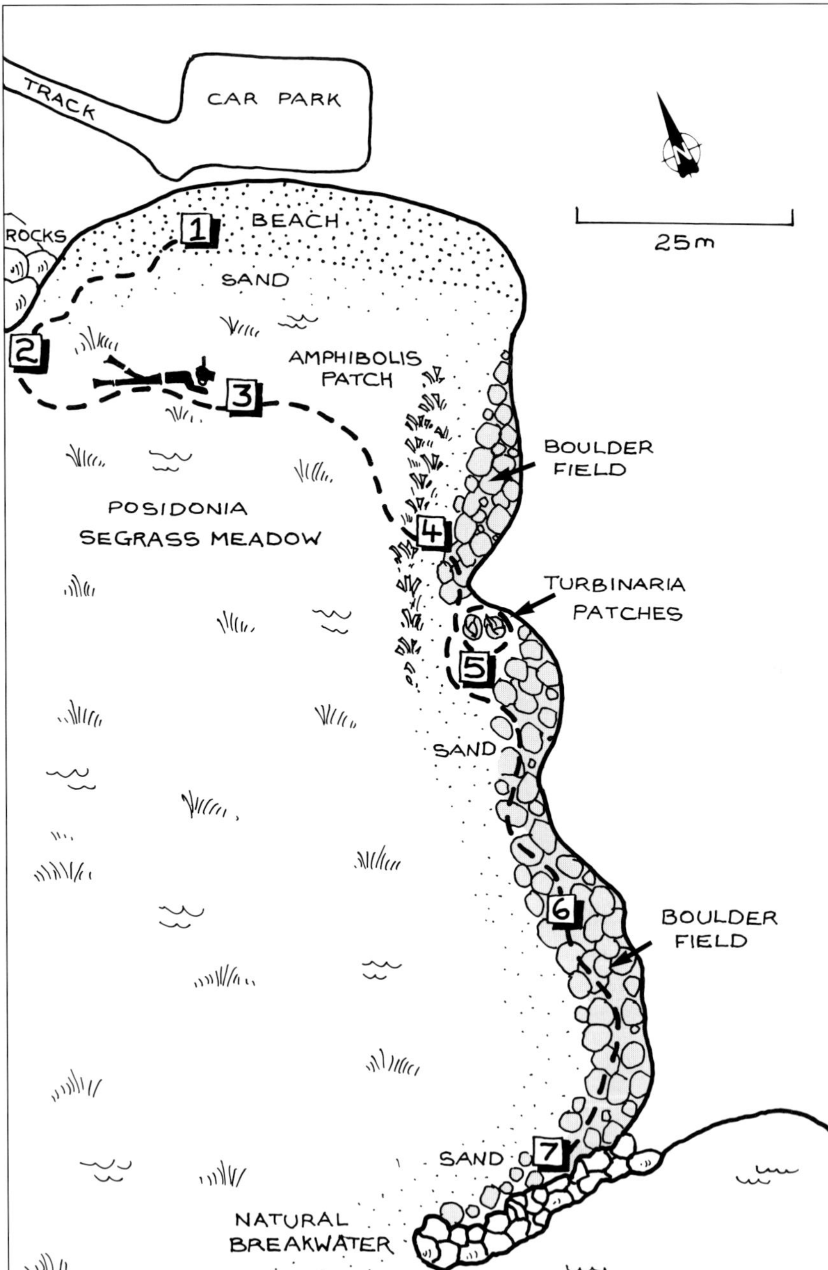

TRACK
CAR PARK
BEACH
ROCKS
SAND
25m
AMPHIBOLIS PATCH
BOULDER FIELD
POSIDONIA SEGRASS MEADOW
TURBINARIA PATCHES
SAND
BOULDER FIELD
SAND
NATURAL BREAKWATER
1
2
3
4
5
6
7

Little Boat Harbour, Bremer Bay

How to get there: *By car from Bremer Bay.*
Depth: *2-8 metres.*

To reach Little Boat Harbour, drive about 9 km south from Bremer Bay on the road to Point Henry and turn right down to Dillon Bay. If you have a four-wheel-drive, park in the small car park at the bottom of the hill, otherwise park in the car park above Little Boat Harbour. This site, on the eastern edge of Dillon Bay, is very sheltered from the easterly and south-easterly winds that blow across the South Coast in summer. It is suitable for novice and more experienced snorkellers and is a relatively easy shore dive on SCUBA.

1. Swim off the small sandy beach and bear right towards the rocks. Stingrays often lurk on the sand between the beach and the start of the seagrass bed.
2. The little granite headland at this end of the beach is an interesting spot to explore at the start of your swim.
3. As you cross the extensive meadow of ribbon weed seagrass (*Posidonia*), keep a lookout amongst the fronds for the spectacular common seadragon. This amazingly coloured fish is one of two species of seadragon found in the temperate waters around Western Australia's coastline. You may also spot the varied cat shark hiding amongst the seagrass. This species is easily recognised by its sinuous shape and white-spotted black collar just behind the head.
4. Closer to the rocks, on the left hand side of the beach, there is a small patch of wireweed (*Amphibolis*) seagrass. Rainbow fish sometimes shelter in the seagrass and adjacent beds of seaweed. The males of this species are, as the name suggests, very brightly coloured, whereas the females are dull and more difficult to spot, as they blend in with the seagrass fronds. The seagrass beds are also home to a number of different leatherjackets.
5. There is an extensive granite boulder field adjacent to the shore. The rocky sea bed is largely covered in kelp and other seaweeds, apart from the shaded sides and overhangs of some of the larger boulders. Swimming along the shoreline, you will come across two large patches of cabbage coral (*Turbinaria*). These multistorey structures shelter a variety of fish, including bullseyes, attractive black-headed pullers and old wives. A diverse range of invertebrates also live on or around these colonies, such as the dusky pink coloured basket star (*Astroboa ernae*), which

can be found during the day under the coral plates, with their long arms folded up into a basket.

6. On the upper surfaces of the boulders, there are several large colonies of the bright green zoanthid (*Zoanthus praelongus*), which resembles an anemone. In the holes between the boulders you may come across blue-spotted pufferfish, which will usually follow you around for a while. Blue-spotted goatfish often frequent a strip of sand between the edge of the boulder field and the seagrass beds.

As you swim towards the end of the natural breakwater, the water becomes more turbulent. Schools of silver drummer and trevally are common in this area. Occasionally, during the late summer and autumn, large schools of salmon sometimes swim into Little Boat Harbour from the open waters of Dillon Bay.

Caution areas: *Only swim around the end of the natural breakwater in the calmest conditions, as there is little protection from the swell on the other side of it.*
Degree of difficulty: *Easy to moderate.*

Jeremy Colman

ALBANY TO DENMARK

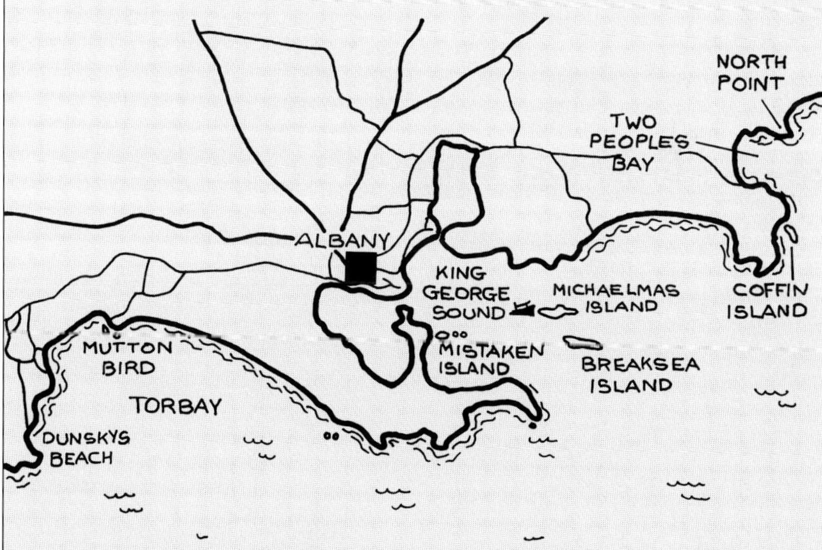

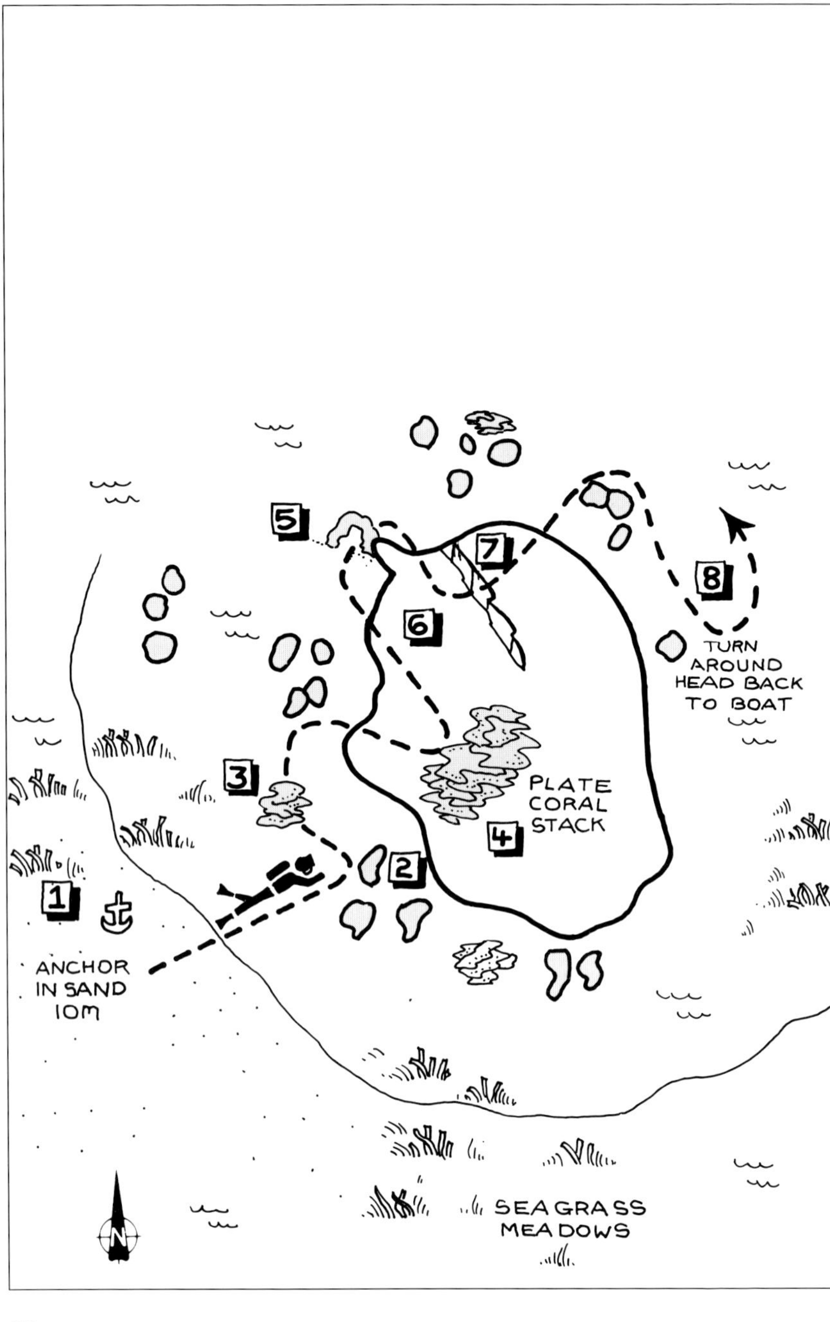

5
7
6
8
TURN
AROUND
HEAD BACK
TO BOAT
3
PLATE
CORAL
STACK
4
2
1
ANCHOR
IN SAND
10m
N
SEAGRASS
MEADOWS

South Point, Two Peoples Bay

9

How to get there: *By small boat from the boat launching area at Two Peoples Bay.*
Depth: *8-10 metres.*

Two Peoples Bay Nature Reserve has excellent barbecue facilities, with a large grassed picnic area with plenty of shade. There are toilet facilities, but no camping or dogs are allowed. First Reef, or Ten Metre Reef, is about halfway across the bay towards South Point, looking straight out from Two Peoples Bay. It is a dive best done in westerly or north-westerly winds and can be good for snorkelling on a clear day. To get to the dive site, travel by car from Albany along Lower King Road and turn left at the Two Peoples Bay sign. Continue along Two Peoples Bay Road (unsealed gravel) until you reach the beach. There is a boat launching area off the white sandy beach. Travel by boat a short distance across the bay, heading towards South Point, until you see a small rock which breaks at the surface.

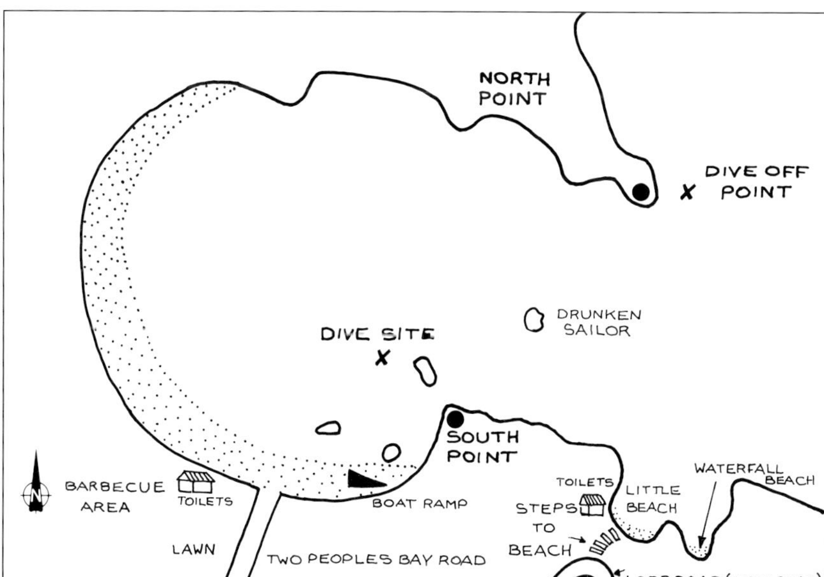

1. Anchor in the sand on the north-western side of the rock. The site is a circular complex of granite boulders covered with marine life and colourful sponges. There is a sandy bottom with seagrass meadows. Swim towards the reef.
2. You will come across jumbled rocks covered with sponges, sea stars, brittle stars and sea cucumbers.
3. As you swim in a clockwise direction, you will see small singular plate corals, with small schools of black-headed pullers, wrasse and bicolor scalyfins.
4. One of the highlights of this reef is a large formation of plate coral, which is stacked up high. As you swim over and around it, look in all the cracks and small hiding spots, and you will see all kinds of marine inhabitants, such as shrimps, gobies, boxfish and pufferfish. There are usually large schools of black-headed pullers.
5. Continue towards the sand line and you will come across a small archway, home to a western blue devil and schools of old wives. Take time to look in rock crevices and under low-lying boulders. If you are lucky you will find an octopus. These creatures are timid, shy and quite harmless.
6. Throughout the dive you will see various fish, such as harlequin fish, bullseyes, western foxfish, maori wrasse, red-lipped morwongs and queen snapper. A large black resident ray often comes to see what's happening.
7. The next point of interest is a large rock, about five metres tall, which slopes gently towards the surface. Look along the crevice, which is home to bullseyes, swallowtails and cuttlefish. It is known as "Cuttlefish Ledge", as during the breeding season, usually between April and June, they can become a bit over-friendly and may follow you around. Dazzle them with your torch and they will come out to investigate. The crevice is also home to graceful western blue devils.
8. The north-eastern end of the reef becomes plainer, with scattered outcrops of smaller boulders, and the sponge and fish life becomes more widespread. You can turn around here and swim back to your starting point.

Caution areas: *Do not dive this site in a swell of more than 1.5 metres. It then becomes too surgy and the visibility is poor.*
Degree of difficulty: *In the right weather conditions this is an excellent site for newly certified to experienced divers. It is ideal for small boats.*
Area's status: *The waters of Two Peoples Bay are in a proposed marine reserve.*

Michelle Hands

OCTOPUSES

The name octopus comes from Octopoda, which means "eight-footed". All octopuses have eight arms. They are molluscs and, along with their close relatives the squids and cuttlefish, are the most highly developed invertebrates, with a well developed brain and eye structure.

Octopuses have no hard parts, except the beak. When disturbed or attacked, these animals will eject a cloud of ink in order to distract the predator, so they can escape. They usually crawl along the sea floor, but can swim for short distances by forcing water through their bodies. Usually well camouflaged, octopuses can change colour to merge into their surroundings. They are bottom-dwellers and secrete themselves under rocks and other debris and in crevices. A pile of recently dead shells is usually a tell-tale sign of their lair. Most octopuses have short lives and only survive for a year or so.

One small, but colourful, creature to be wary of is the blue-ringed octopus. It kills its prey with a potent toxin injected with the bite, and, although such cases are very rare, has killed people. The toxin causes paralysis and respiratory failure. Blue-ringed octopuses grow up to 12 centimetres across, living in reef flats and tidal pools. They can be recognised by their brilliant blue rings when disturbed. Be cautious when handling dead shells, or discarded cans and bottles, and when exploring tidal pools or underwater crevices and caves. If you are unlucky enough to be bitten you should keep the injured limb still, put direct pressure on the wound and seek medical aid urgently.

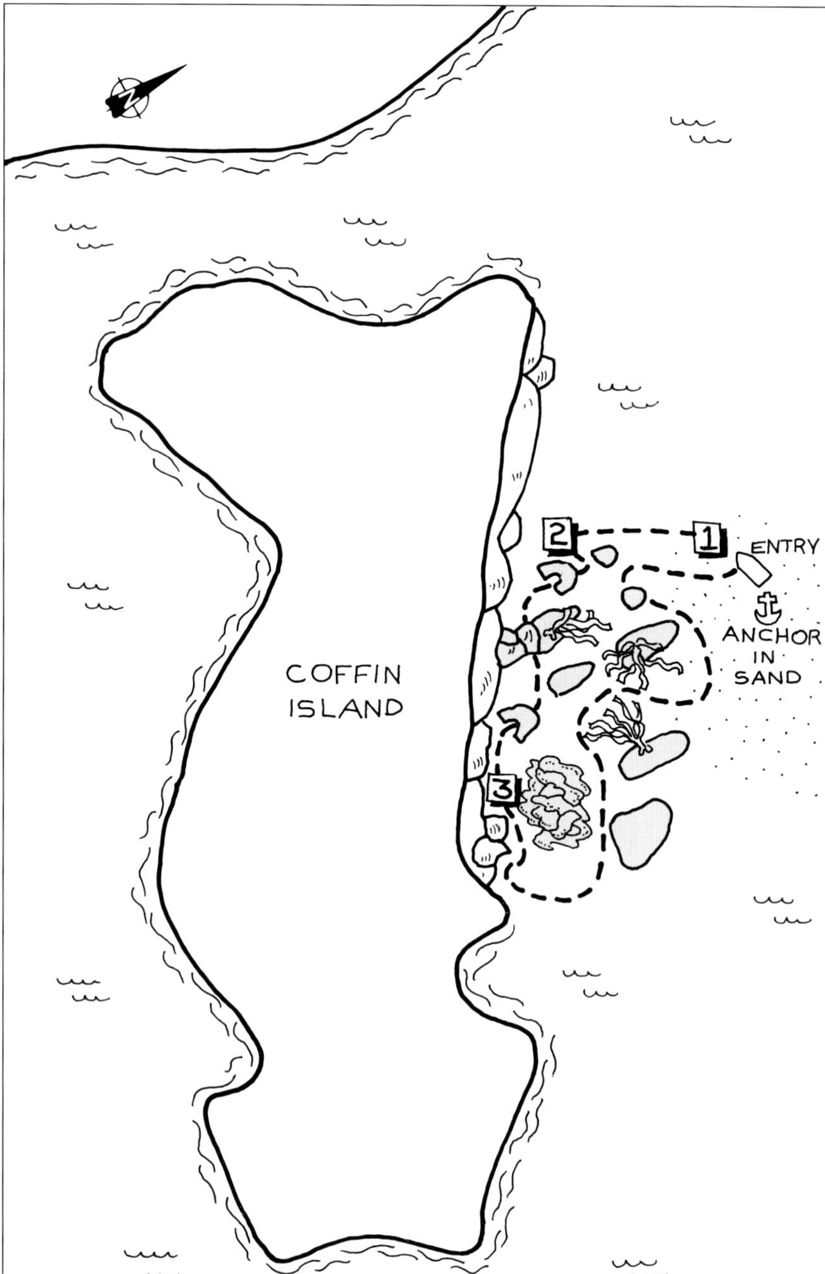
COFFIN ISLAND
2
1
ENTRY
ANCHOR IN SAND
3

Coffin Island, Two Peoples Bay

10

How to get there: *By small boat from the boat launching area at Two Peoples Bay.*
Depth: *12-18 metres.*

Two Peoples Bay Nature Reserve has excellent barbecue facilities, with a large grassed picnic area with plenty of shade. There are toilet facilities, but no camping or dogs are allowed. Coffin Island is an easy boat dive for beginners to intermediate level. The site is best dived in light southerly winds, with a swell of one metre or less. Take a good dive torch and camera, as this is an excellent site for underwater photography and macro photography. To reach the site, travel by car from Albany along Lower King Road and Two Peoples Bay Road (unsealed gravel). There is a boat launching area off the white sandy beach. Travel by boat out of the Bay, heading around the right hand side to Coffin Island.

1. Anchor in the sand towards the north-western end of the island, where the depth is about 18 metres. The dive site consists of numerous small and larger caves. Inside these caves are schools of bullseyes, swallowtails and various types of fish. The cave walls are covered with a myriad of colourful sponges.
2. There are large granite rock bombies along the sand line. The sides of these bombies are covered with all types of soft corals, large white gorgonian fan corals, sponges and sea squirts. The tops of bombies in shallower water are covered with kelp. There is a good variety of fish life in the area, such as blue gropers, huge silver drummers, queen snapper, brightly coloured harlequin fish, western foxfish and other smaller varieties, such as black-headed pullers.
3. Between the rock bombies and cave structures, you will come across a large plate coral formation surrounded by white sand. This is magical to see on a bright, sunny day, as it is very picturesque. You also have a good chance of seeing a seal underwater, as they rest nearby.

Caution areas: *Swimming into caves can be hazardous in surge. Wobbegongs and cuttlefish can be over-friendly. Take potential wind changes into account when anchoring your vessel.*
Degree of difficulty: *Easy to moderate, depending on conditions.*
Area's status: *The waters of Two Peoples Bay are in a proposed marine reserve.*

Steven Hands

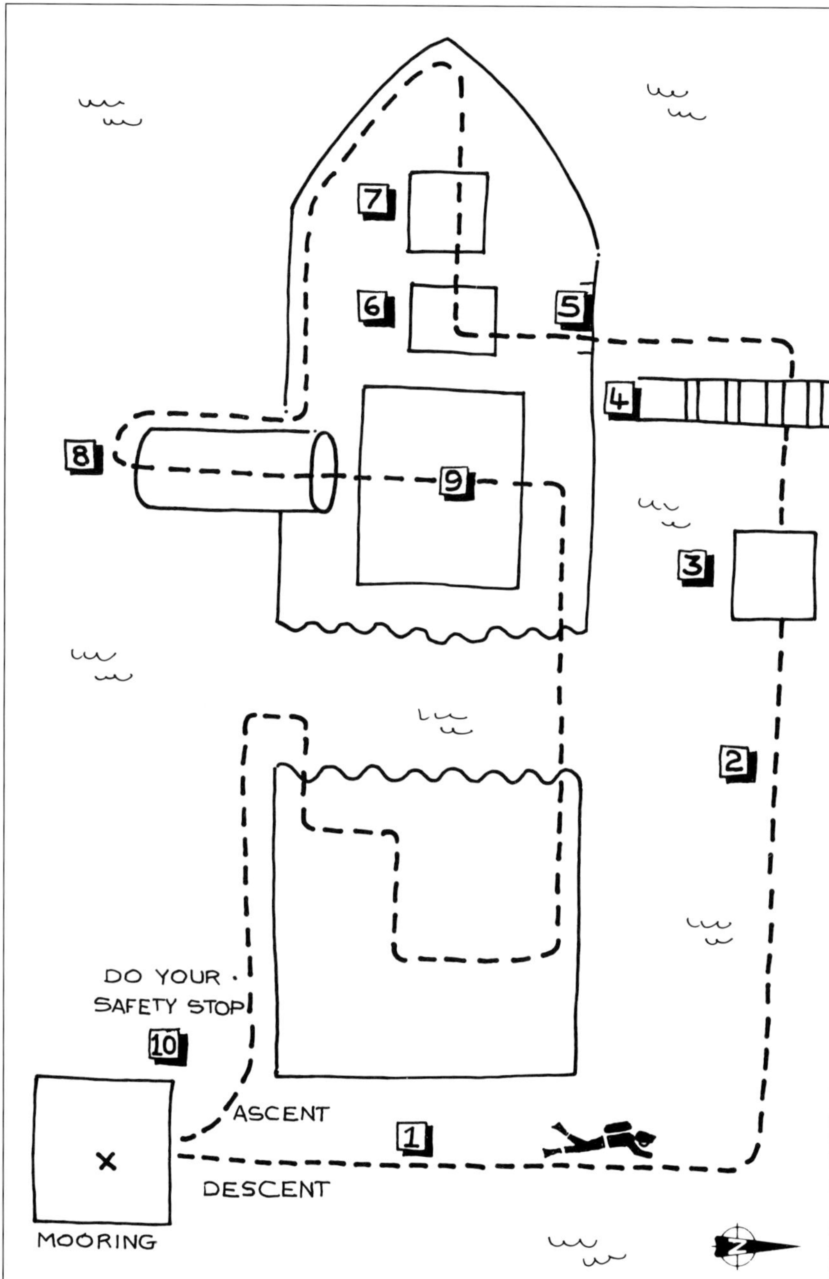
7
6
5
4
8
9
3
2
DO YOUR
SAFETY STOP
10
ASCENT
1
DESCENT
MOORING
N

Cheynes III wreck

How to get there: *By boat from Emu Point.*
Depth: *12 metres on deck to 23 metres in sand. However, the deepest divers will usually get is 18 metres.*

Follow the channel markers out of Emu Point into King George Sound. Head out in an easterly direction to Michaelmas Island, where you will find a mooring on the western end. The wreck's position is indicated by a large mooring which has a bright yellow buoy, marked "*Cheynes III*". The beauty of this wreck is that it can be dived in most weather conditions, due to the protection of the island. It is especially good in summer, when the easterly winds make most other dive sites around Albany inaccessible. The *Cheynes III* is teeming with fish and encrusted with colourful sponges and marine life. Take a torch for below the deck.

The *Cheynes III* was sunk by the South Coast Divers Club on June 23 1982, to provide a recreational dive site. It is the only one of its kind with no commercial affiliations and lies in an upright position on a sandy bottom. The *Cheynes III* was built in England in 1947 and was bought by the local whaling station after the closure of a Queensland whaling company. The 440 ton ship was 157 feet long, and fitted with a Norwegian whale gun, which fired a harpoon with an explosive head, attached to 45 fathoms of line used to winch the whale back to the ship. However, due to the increased pressure from conservation groups and the depressed market for whale oil, the Cheynes Beach Whaling Co. decided in July 1978 to cease operations at the end of the season. The last whale was taken at Albany on November 20, 1978. This marked the end of an era for Albany. We can now enjoy seeing the humpback and southern right whales that visit our coastline each year.

1. Descend down the mooring line, and head north towards the stern, where you will find the rudder and propeller partially buried in the sand.
2. Follow along the right hand side of the vessel, where you will be greeted by a myriad of fish life, ranging from gropers, boarfish, old wives, queen snapper, harlequin fish, skippy and black-headed pullers.
3. Continue on, where you pass by a broken section of the wreck. Nearby is a plaque. Clean the plaque and have a read. The stirring up will attract wrasse and other fish. After 15 years of being exposed to the elements, the hull has broken about midway along the ship, just behind the main superstructure of the wheel house, and it has developed more of a list to the port. However, it is still in reasonable condition.

4. The old hand rail can be seen from the deck.
5. Enter through the side of the vessel and you will see a large school of bullseyes and swallowtails. Occasionally, you will see a western blue devil.
6. Exit out of the deck hatch, to continue forward to the powder room. Inspect the growth. The wreck has a good coverage of marine invertebrates, sponges, bryozoans, telesto corals and anemones, all supporting a multitude of other animals, such as crabs, shrimps, shells, nudibranchs, triple fins and gobies.
7. You may enter the powder room, but first inspect it for a large resident wobbegong. If it's there don't enter, as it gets upset.
8. The smoke stack is now lying on its side, with most of it hanging over the edge. You can swim through it in single file, but it easily stirs up.
9. The cabin and lower decks, which are covered in colourful soft corals, can be closely inspected. You may find some western blue devils hiding and large queen snapper swimming by. It is still possible to swim along the companionways and explore the different levels from the bridge to the lower deck, then forward to the bow, passing winches and other machinery.
10. Ascend slowly up the mooring line and remember to do your safety stop.

There is nothing like diving the wreck on a clear day, and just viewing the entire ship. Its ever-present schools of fish mill around the various ramparts and the sun highlights the rails, ladders and other structural features of the vessel.

Caution areas: *Do not swim into the powder room without looking for the wobbegong first. Beware of boat traffic. Take care when swimming in and out of openings, as silting can occur.*
Degree of difficulty: *Due to its depth, this is a site for qualified advanced divers only.*
Area's status: *The waters around Michaelmas Island are in a proposed marine reserve. There is a "no fish" zone for 100 metres around the wreck.*

Steven Hands

CONESHELLS

Coneshells may bury themselves in sand, with only their snorkel-like siphon extended. Some are reported to shoot out their harpoon-like teeth, like a dart, or they may leap out to stab a fast-moving fish. A number of these detachable teeth are stored inside the body ready for use. The powerful venom injected with the barb paralyses the prey and the coneshell proceeds to devour its meal. Eight species of coneshell in northern Australia are known to be or thought to be poisonous. However, these nocturnal animals are rarely seen and usually only bite in self-defence, when people are trying to remove a live animal for its beautiful shell.

The huge number of species (more than 300) are found in a great variety of decorative patterns and vary greatly in size. Depending on the species, coneshells may reach up to 10 centimetres long. By day, coneshells bury themselves in sand and usually emerge at night in search of small fish, snails or worms.

While not all coneshells are dangerous, it is far better to be wary of all species. The probiscus from which the poison harpoons are shot can become very long very quickly, striking a finger regardless of where the animal is held. Symptoms may include numbness, swelling and pain and, in the case of the geographer cone, even death. If someone is bitten, immobilise the injured area and seek immediate medical attention. Be prepared to apply mouth-to -mouth resuscitation to the victim if breathing failure appears likely.

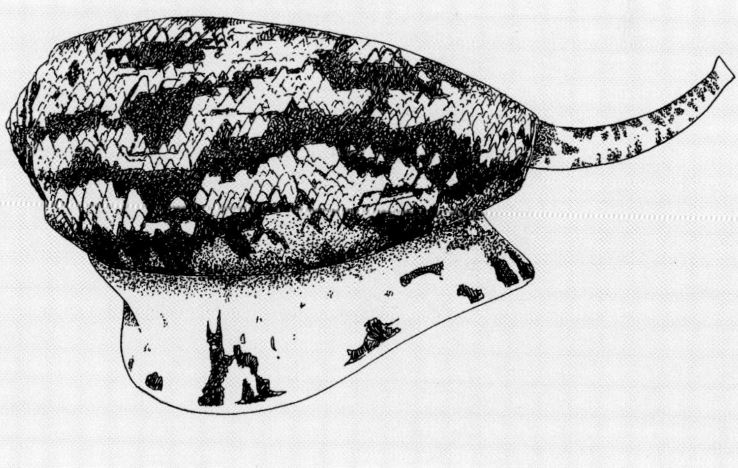

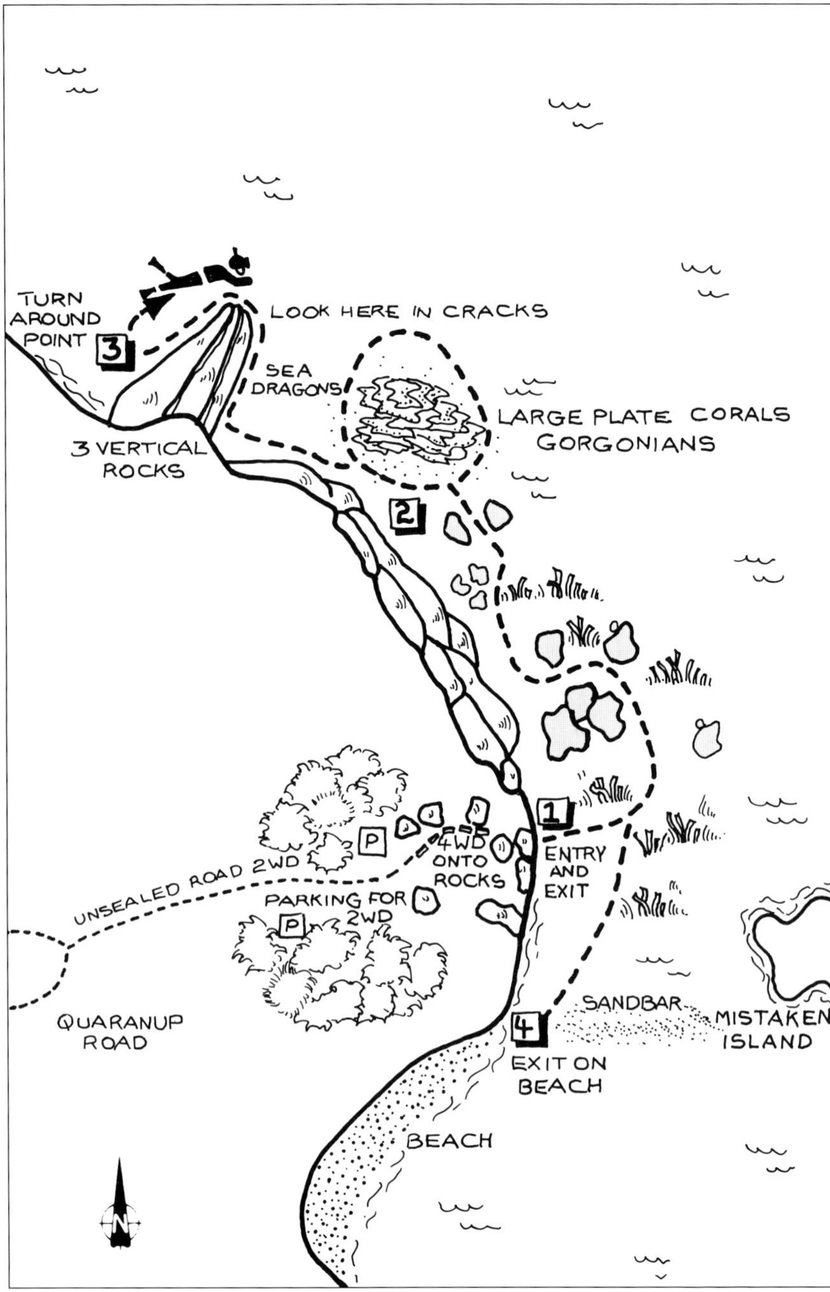
TURN AROUND POINT
3
LOOK HERE IN CRACKS
SEA DRAGONS
LARGE PLATE CORALS
GORGONIANS
3 VERTICAL ROCKS
2
1
P
4WD ONTO ROCKS
ENTRY AND EXIT
UNSEALED ROAD 2WD
PARKING FOR 2WD
P
SANDBAR
4
MISTAKEN ISLAND
QUARANUP ROAD
EXIT ON BEACH
BEACH
N

Mistaken Island

How to get there: *Travel by car from Albany along Frenchmans Bay Road (sealed). Turn left onto Quaranup Road (2WD limestone). Travel about 1 km, then turn right near the hairpin bend. Park in a small area near rocks.*
Depth: *7-11 metres.*

This shore dive has very good entry and exit points, is relatively easy to navigate and the keen-eyed can usually spot common seadragons. It would also make an excellent night dive. Mistaken Island is a good dive when the wind is offshore. Only dive it in westerly winds when the swell is less than one metre.

1. Entry is from a large flat rock. Swim to the left of the rocks and follow the shoreline, swimming initially over seagrass and sandy bottom. Gradually undulating slopes are covered with bright orange and yellow sponges. Colonies of blue and white ascidians are scattered along some smaller rocks, with sea urchins, sea squirts, sea cucumbers, sea stars, feather stars and hydroids inhabiting the cracks and crevices. Maori wrasse, leatherjackets and boxfish will follow as you stir up the sand. There are also smaller types of fish life, bullseyes, swallowtails, black-headed pullers and a large black ray that often passes by.
2. Towards the point of the shoreline, you will come across a small rocky outcrop, a low-lying rock bombie surrounded by sand. This picturesque area is covered with small orange, brown, yellow and red gorgonian fan corals, black and yellow bryozoans, large ascidians and plate coral on top. All sorts of tiny creatures live in the nooks and crannies, including brittle stars, crabs, shrimps and gobies.
3. Not far ahead, you will come across a small rock formation, with three large crevices that run into 12 metres of water. Common seadragons camouflage themselves well by hiding amongst the kelp in these crevices. They can be easily seen on a night dive as they come out of the weed.
4. Turn around and follow the shoreline back. You may exit via the flat rocks, or swim a little further south to exit via the white sandy beach.

Caution areas: *Be careful of the barnacles on the flat rocks. The site should not be dived if water is surgy or in rough weather conditions. Use a large dive flag in this area, as it is subject to boat traffic.*
Degree of difficulty: *Easy to moderate shore dive, depending on conditions.*
Area's status: *The waters around Mistaken Island are in a proposed marine reserve.*

Michelle Hands

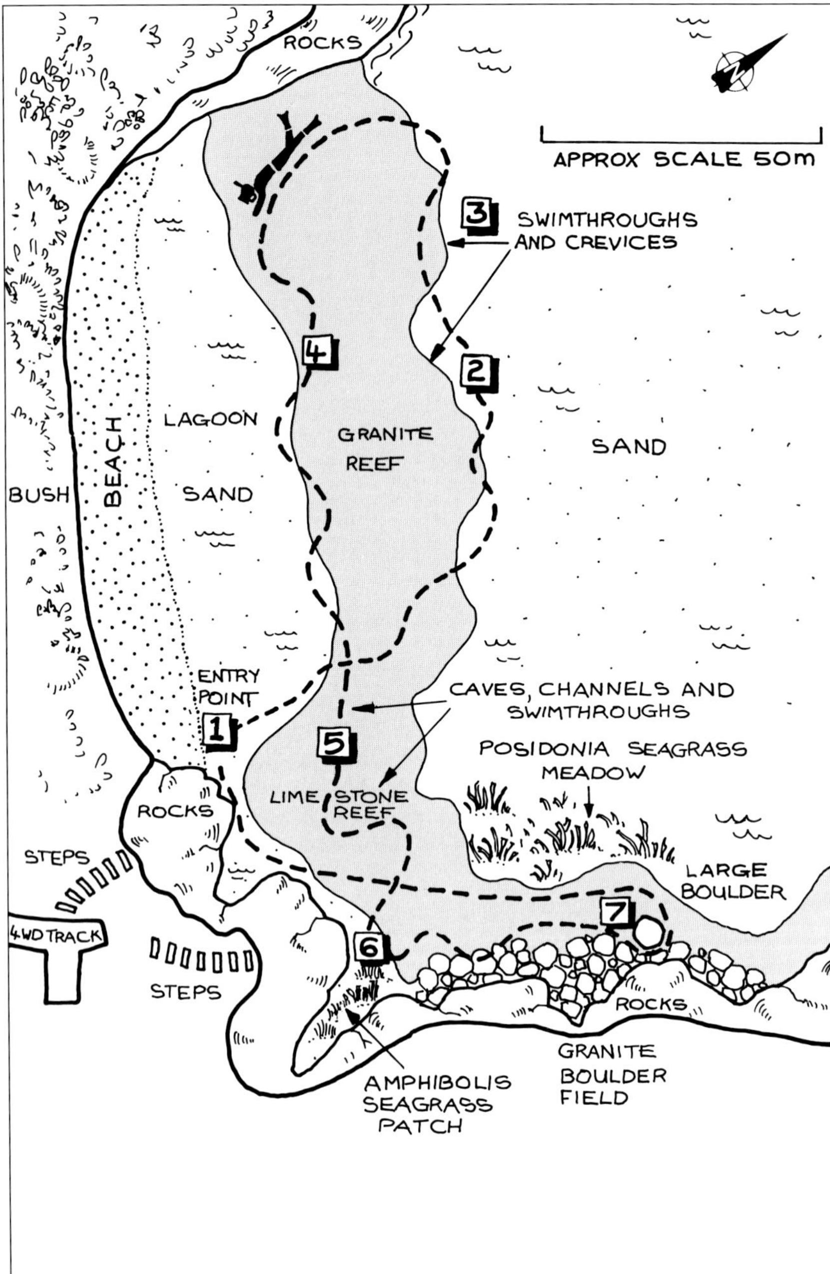
ROCKS
APPROX SCALE 50m
3
SWIMTHROUGHS AND CREVICES
4
2
LAGOON
GRANITE REEF
SAND
BUSH
BEACH
SAND
ENTRY POINT
1
CAVES, CHANNELS AND SWIMTHROUGHS
5
POSIDONIA SEAGRASS MEADOW
LIME STONE REEF
ROCKS
STEPS
LARGE BOULDER
7
4WD TRACK
6
STEPS
ROCKS
GRANITE BOULDER FIELD
AMPHIBOLIS SEAGRASS PATCH

Dunsky Beach

How to get there: *By 4WD from Denmark or Albany, or by boat from Cosy Corner or Shelley Beach.*
Depth: *2-8 metres.*

Even though land access to Dunsky Beach is restricted to four-wheel-drive vehicles, it is still one of the most popular dive sites near Albany. The sheltered location and an interesting combination of granite and limestone reef provide excellent snorkelling and diving opportunities for both novices and the more experienced. To reach the site, turn off the lower Denmark to Albany Road onto Cosy Corner Road and drive south into West Cape Howe National Park. A four-wheel-drive track (Dunsky Road) leads off Shelley Beach Road on the right hand side, about one kilometre before you get to Shelley Beach. The track runs south towards West Cape Howe for about four kilometres, before reaching a turn-off on the left. Follow this track for about two kilometres to Dunsky Beach. Dunsky Beach is also accessible by small boats, which can be launched either from Cosy Corner or Shelley Beach.

1. The easiest entry point is from the southern corner of the beach, next to the rocks at the end of the vehicle track. A wide band of reef extends across the small bay, parallel to the beach. Swim over the reef and head north towards the rocks at the far end of the beach. As you cross the kelp-covered rocks you are likely to spot a variety of fish amongst the seaweed fronds, including herring cale and sea carp.
2. The seaward side of the reef drops to a sandy bottom at about 6 to 8 metres and is quite broken, with numerous boulders, crevices and ledges. Under the ledges and covering some of the vertical walls is a profusion of encrusting life, with colourful sponges, sea squirts, fan corals and soft corals. Several species of sea star feed on these invertebrates, including a bright orange species and a red sea star with a soft, velvety appearance.
3. A wide variety of fish inhabit the caves, swimthroughs and crevices in this area, including schools of rough bullseyes, yellow-headed prettyfins, black-headed pullers and Woodward's pomfret. Larger fish, such as western blue groper, dusky morwong and queen snapper, also swim between the rocks on the reef front. Western wirrah and the spectacular western blue devil hide in caves and under ledges. Out in open water you may spot schools of herring and trevally.
4. When you reach the rocks at the far end of the bay, turn inshore and head across the reef towards the beach. As you swim along the inner reef edge, you will come

across a number of ledges which are usually home to schools of old wives, one of the most common and characteristic fish of our temperate waters. Senator wrasse and horseshoe leatherjackets also frequent this area.

5. As you swim south, the reef changes from granite to limestone. The bottom flattens out and has less seaweed cover, but is honeycombed with holes, swimthroughs, caves and long channels that are narrow at the top and widen towards the sea bed. Zebra fish, red-lipped morwong and maori wrasse are common. The caves are home to bullseyes, scalyfins, moonlighters and goatfish, while sponges, hydroids, sea squirts and patches of red and orange gorgonians cover the walls. Slate pencil urchins are often wedged beneath ledges.
6. In the southern corner of the bay is a small patch of wireweed (*Amphibolis*) seagrass where you may see several Brownfield's wrasse, a small green fish with iridescent spots and stripes. In deeper water on the sandy bottom there are larger areas of seagrass, mainly ribbon weed (*Posidonia* species). As you swim round the large granite boulders fringing the shoreline, the sea bed changes again from limestone to a granite boulder field. Silver drummers, banded sweep and sea sweep will often follow you. On some boulders there are large patches of a bright green zoanthid, a colonial animal that resembles small anemones. They feed mainly at night and retract their tentacles during the day.
7. About halfway along the bay's southern shore is a large granite boulder that rises to within a couple of metres of the surface. One side of this boulder is covered with colonies of bryozoans, which form folded orange calcareous clumps resembling corals.

Caution areas: *Take care as you carry heavy gear down the rocks to the beach. Swimming under ledges and into swimthroughs can be hazardous.*
Degree of difficulty: *Easy to moderate.*
Area's status: *The waters adjacent to West Cape Howe National Park are a proposed marine reserve.*

Jeremy Colman

BOTTLENOSE DOLPHIN

Bottlenose dolphins abound in Western Australian waters. Take some time to look carefully over the water surface and you may see these magnificent creatures riding on the bow wave created by boats, or cruising through the water. These air breathing mammals must periodically surface to breath through the blow hole on the top of the head. The dolphin has a grey back but its belly is a light grey colour. This countershading helps to camouflage the animal. As potential predators, such as sharks, look up from the deep, the light grey belly blends in with bright surface waters. Seen from above, the grey back blends in with the deep dark waters below. Bottlenose dolphins vary greatly in size, depending on where they are found. Average length is three metres and calves are about a metre at birth.

This species is common in cold, temperate and tropical seas and estuaries all over the world. It is often seen close inshore, even entering rivers, and an offshore form is found in the open ocean. Bottlenose dolphins have a complex yet fascinating social structure. Within a population, they form small subgroups which inhabit a defined home range. Members of a group, however, may change from time to time and they assist each other in activities such as fish herding and calf rearing. Even mating is a group activity the males co-operate to herd a female in reproductive condition and take turns to mate with her. They also try to prevent rival groups from having access to her. A calf is generally born 12 months later. Bottlenose dolphins eat a wide variety of fish, squid and octopuses. The offshore form may be able to dive to depths of more than 600 metres to catch food.

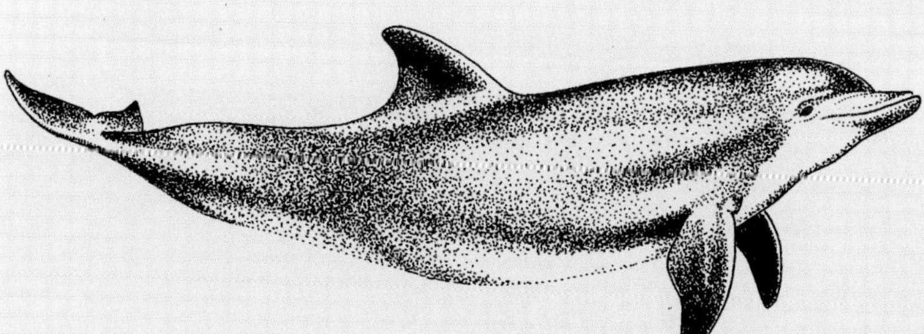

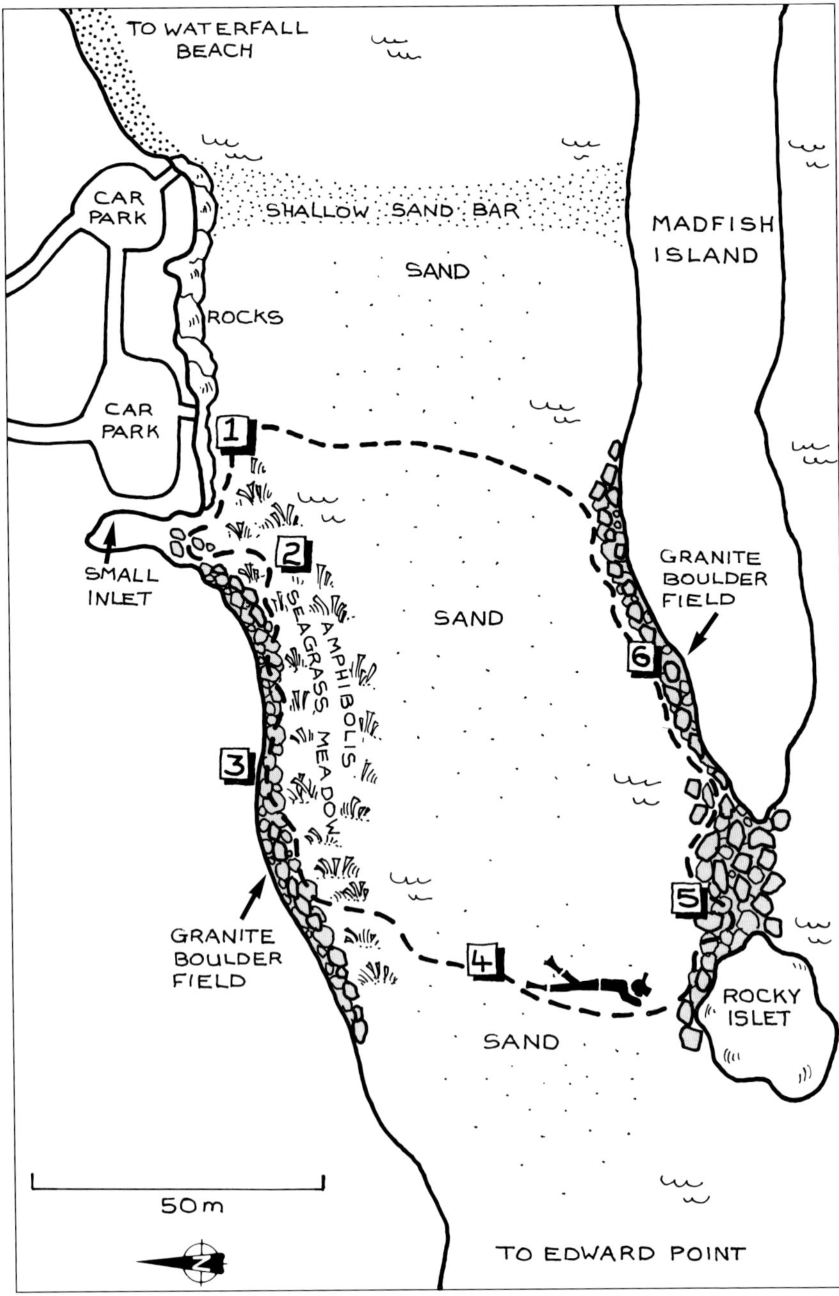
TO WATERFALL BEACH
CAR PARK
SHALLOW SAND BAR
MADFISH ISLAND
SAND
ROCKS
CAR PARK
1
2
SMALL INLET
SAND
AMPHIBOLIS SEAGRASS MEADOW
GRANITE BOULDER FIELD
6
3
5
GRANITE BOULDER FIELD
4
ROCKY ISLET
SAND
50m
TO EDWARD POINT

Madfish Bay

How to get there: *By car from Denmark or Albany.*
Depth: *2-6 metres.*

The shallow, protected waters of the channel between Madfish Island and the mainland provide a sheltered spot for snorkelling, or for novice SCUBA divers. The visibility is generally very good and the granite boulder areas, seagrass meadows and sand patches support a wide variety of fish species. To reach Madfish Bay, turn left off the South Coast Highway, about 12 kilometres west of Denmark, and drive south for four kilometres into William Bay National Park. Before you reach Greens Pool, turn left onto Madfish Bay Road and follow the road east for about two kilometres towards Madfish Bay. Turn right before you reach Waterfall Beach and park in the lower car park.

1. Enter the water from the rocks below the car park and swim west along the shoreline. The large granite boulders in the shallows of the small inlet are home to a variety of fish, such as the horseshoe leatherjacket and the black and white striped moonlighter.
2. A meadow of wireweed (*Amphibolis*) seagrass extends across the northern side of the channel, providing shelter for toothbrush leatherjackets. The male has a characteristic set of bristles on each side of the rear of the body, hence its curious name. Small schools of silverbellies are also common in and around seagrass meadows, and you may see Brownfield's wrasse, a small bright green fish that is well camouflaged amongst the seagrass fronds. Keep an eye open for the pretty polly wrasse, a light coloured fish with broken black bars across its body. It swims with a strange erratic motion, with its body positioned diagonally to the sea bed.
3. A narrow area of boulders extends west along the shoreline, towards Edward Point. The medium to large granite boulders are predominantly covered with a variety of brown seaweeds. The nooks and crannies between the boulders provide excellent shelter for several common temperate reef fish, such as maori wrasse, brown-spotted wrasse, black-spotted wrasse, old wives and herring cale. Look closely in some of the larger holes and you may spot the western rock blackfish, which is bluish-black with a mottled appearance. In open water above the boulders you may also come across zebra fish, a closely related species.
4. Blue-spotted goatfish are common on the sandy bottom between the boulder field and the seagrass meadow. As you swim south across the sand, towards the

rocky islet off the western end of Madfish Island, look out for flatheads sitting on the sand and schools of herring swimming past.

5. Numerous invertebrates shelter under some of the kelp-covered granite boulders, including gorgonians, sponges, sea squirts and lace corals. McCulloch's scalyfins and common bullseyes inhabit holes between the boulders. The silver drummer, a species that feeds on seaweeds and is generally considered inedible (like the closely-related buffalo bream found on the west coast), and large dusky morwong frequent the area in between the rocky islet and Madfish Island.
6. As you swim across the boulder field on the inside of the island you may spot several senator wrasse, distinctive green fish with reddish stripes along their sides, amongst the kelp and other large seaweeds. Swim back across the channel to the entry point. Schools of King George whiting can often be seen in the channel.

Degree of difficulty: *Easy.*
Area's status: *The waters adjacent to William Bay National Park are a proposed marine reserve.*

Jeremy Colman

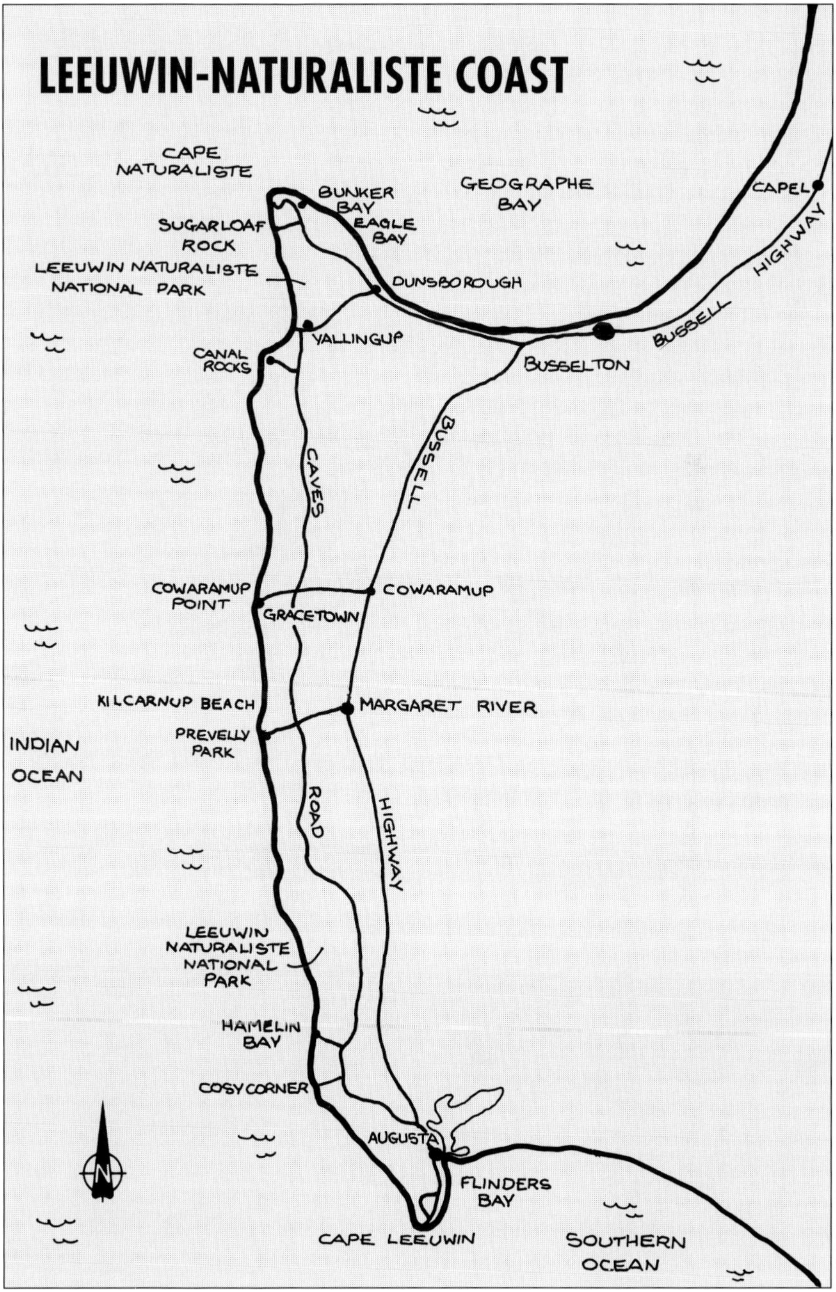
LEEUWIN-NATURALISTE COAST
CAPE NATURALISTE
BUNKER BAY
EAGLE BAY
GEOGRAPHE BAY
CAPEL
SUGARLOAF ROCK
LEEUWIN NATURALISTE NATIONAL PARK
DUNSBOROUGH
BUSSELL HIGHWAY
YALLINGUP
CANAL ROCKS
BUSSELTON
CAVES
BUSSELL
COWARAMUP POINT
COWARAMUP
GRACETOWN
KILCARNUP BEACH
MARGARET RIVER
PREVELLY PARK
INDIAN OCEAN
ROAD
HIGHWAY
LEEUWIN NATURALISTE NATIONAL PARK
HAMELIN BAY
COSY CORNER
AUGUSTA
FLINDERS BAY
CAPE LEEUWIN
SOUTHERN OCEAN
N

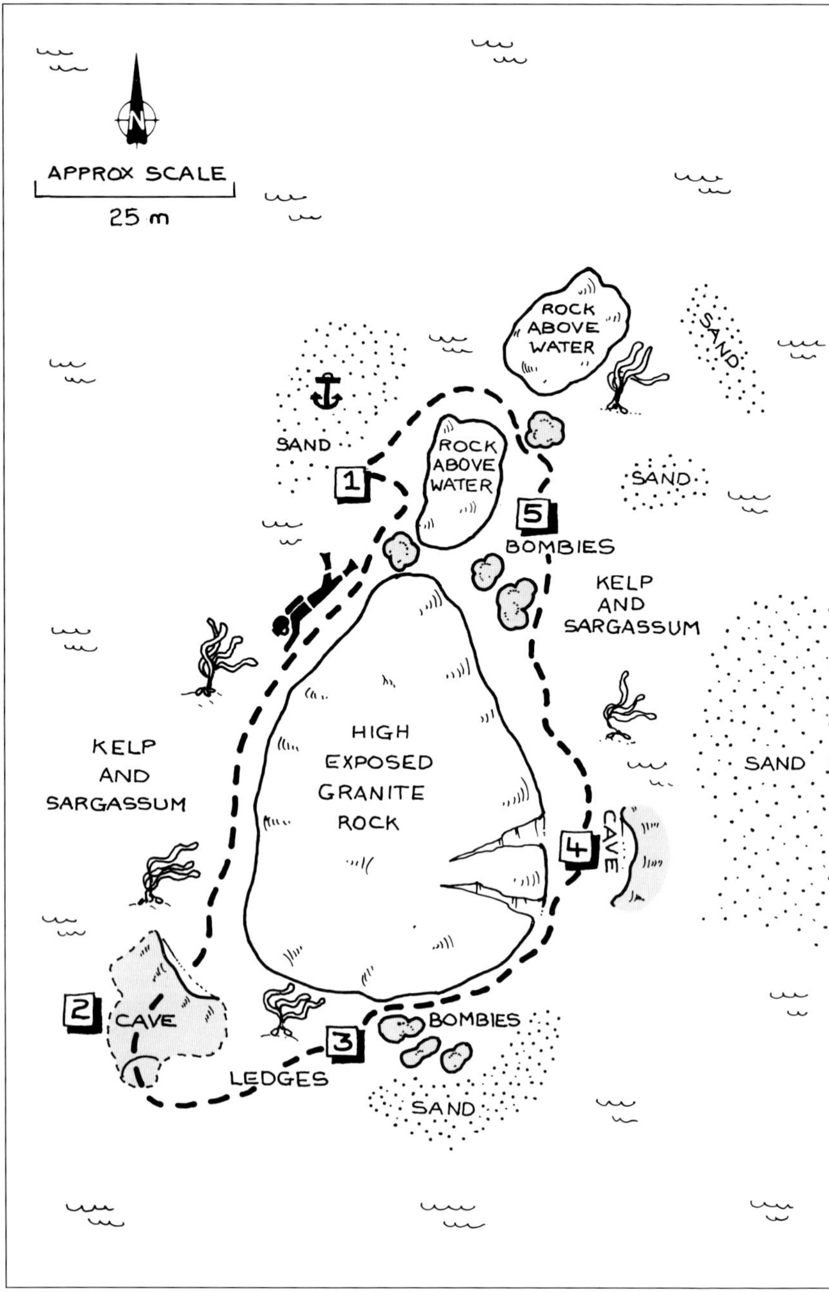
N
APPROX SCALE
25 m
ROCK ABOVE WATER
SAND
SAND
ROCK ABOVE WATER
1
SAND
5
BOMBIES
KELP AND SARGASSUM
HIGH EXPOSED GRANITE ROCK
KELP AND SARGASSUM
SAND
CAVE
4
2
CAVE
BOMBIES
3
LEDGES
SAND

Wrights Rocks

15

How to get there: *By boat from the Flinders Bay boat ramp, south of Augusta.*
Depth: *10-12 metres.*

Wrights Rocks are a tumble of dark-coloured granite rocks rising steeply from the Southern Ocean, 3.7 kilometres south-east of Cape Leeuwin. The GPS co-ordinates are latitude 34° 23.75 south, longitude 115° 09.9 east. There are three main boulders above water level, the largest of which is marked on the RAN Hydrographic Chart as 4.6 metres above sea level. On leaving the entrance to the Flinders Bay boat ramp passage, the rocks are on a true compass bearing of 185° and located six kilometres (3.3 nautical miles) from the boat ramp. This course will take you fairly close to the coast for about the first three kilometres. The boulders are the first in your line of sight and conspicuous on the horizon to the south. The outline of the rocks has a defined slope away to the right to the water line, and a rather steep, almost vertical left face (see below).

There is an interesting cave to explore at location 2 on the diagram. It is recommended that you explore the cave at the beginning of your dive, then complete the dive in accordance with your remaining air supply and local conditions.

1. On reaching the boulders, anchor in the sand patch off the western side of the smaller boulders. As you reach the bottom, your depth gauge should register approximately 10 metres. Under fair to moderate conditions, the waters around these rocks sparkle with clarity even beneath the highly aerated white water around the immediate apron of the rocks. As you cross from sand to weed-covered ocean floor, a delicate green seaweed of feather-like structure dominates

Wrights Rocks looking south as you approach from Flinders Bay:

the fringes of the sand patch. Zebra fish can be seen at this point and, in mid-column, shoals of herring dash by.

2. Swim to the right, following the main rock wall to its south-western corner. On the bottom, off to your right, a low rock ledge appears out of the dense layers of kelp and sargassum. On closer inspection, the ledge opens as a cave entrance. Although a torch is not necessary to explore this cavern, it is suggested that you carry one, as it enhances the colours and enables exploration of the darker corners at the back of the cave. The cave opens up inside to about the size of an average lounge room. Take a minute once inside for your eyes to adjust to the change in light. At the far end, a shaft of light enters the cave through a large hole. This is your exit. Its many ledges and ceiling support a fascinating array of colourful sponges and soft corals. Lobsters secrete themselves in holes, their feelers waving at you nervously. Note how the amount of plant and animal life reduces as you move further away from the light source. When exploring these caves look closely at the floor, as they are sometimes favourite resting places for wobbegongs that tend to blend with their surroundings.
3. On leaving the cave, the light improves and the Southern Ocean surge is evident again. Explore the series of small ledges on the sea floor nearby, where scalyfins, banded sweep, red-lipped morwongs and king wrasse may be seen. The seaward side of the main rock is a high energy area and rich in life. At this point, the sheer vertical face of the southern side of the rock towers some 10 metres towards the surface, where the intertidal rock face is encrusted with large gooseneck barnacles. Its face and base is covered in kelp and sargassum. Look to the surface and shoals of buffalo bream, in company with sea sweep, circle below the sparkling surface. Below, a sea carp might be seen amongst the seaweed.
4. Continue your circumnavigation of the rocks in an anti-clockwise direction. On the eastern side of the main rock, deep cracks in its wall run all the way to the surface. Only metres away, a low ledge on the sea floor opens out at a depth of 11 metres into a shallow cave covered in a rich growth of marine life. The white sandy floor adds a further fascination to the cave, where Port Jackson sharks congregate, shoals of rough bullseyes gather and foxfish may be seen.
5. Follow the rock face to complete your circuit. Striped sea perch pass by as they circle the rocks, while white-barred boxfish and maori wrasse may be seen near the bottom. A number of submerged boulders can also be explored, as you wind your way back to the boat between the smaller granites to conclude a truly rewarding 45 minute dive.

Caution areas: *Access to this site should only be attempted in slight to moderate sea conditions. Surface currents may be present in these areas and should be checked before commencing any dive. Watch for submerged reefs en route.*
Degree of difficulty: *Moderate to difficult, depending on conditions.*
Area's status: *Proposed marine park.*

Peter Lambert and Ted Wright

SEAWEEDS

Seaweeds, or algae, are very simple life forms and are unrelated to seagrasses. Unlike seagrasses, they do not have roots, stems, leaves, flowers or fruit. Roots are unnecessary because the algae are anchored to rocks by holdfasts. They convert sunlight, chemical substances in seawater and carbon dioxide into proteins, fats and carbohydrates by means of photosynthesis, and are an important food source for many fish and invertebrates. They reproduce by means of spores, which are released directly into the water.

These plants take a huge variety of colours and forms. Most people will be familiar with the most common. Sea lettuce stands out with its bright green fronds. It colonises exposed rock platforms, and shallow pools which are only covered at high tide, and occurs throughout the world. Aboriginal people used to prepare and eat this plant. Kelp is the largest and most common seaweed in southern waters. Large groves of it grow on the deep water reefs along our coast and masses of the weed are blown ashore after heavy winter storms. Beachcombers will also be familiar with sargassum, a brown weed that bears small, ball-like floats. Many red algae are calcified, giving them the appearance of rock-like encrustations.

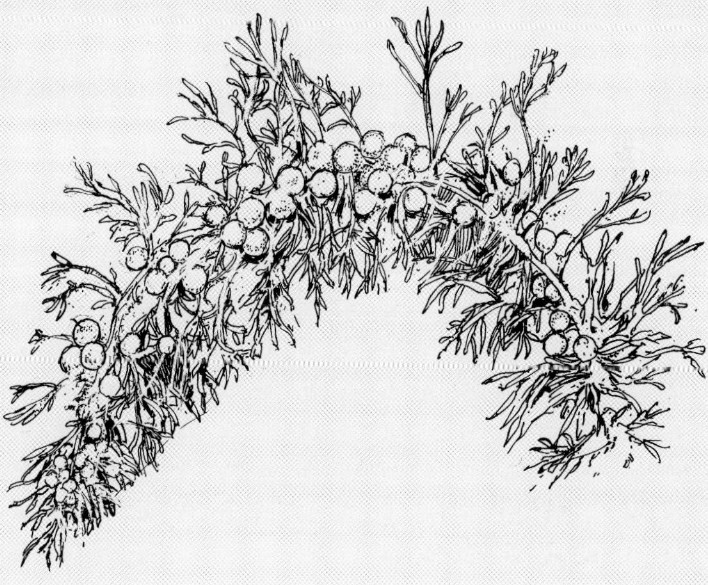

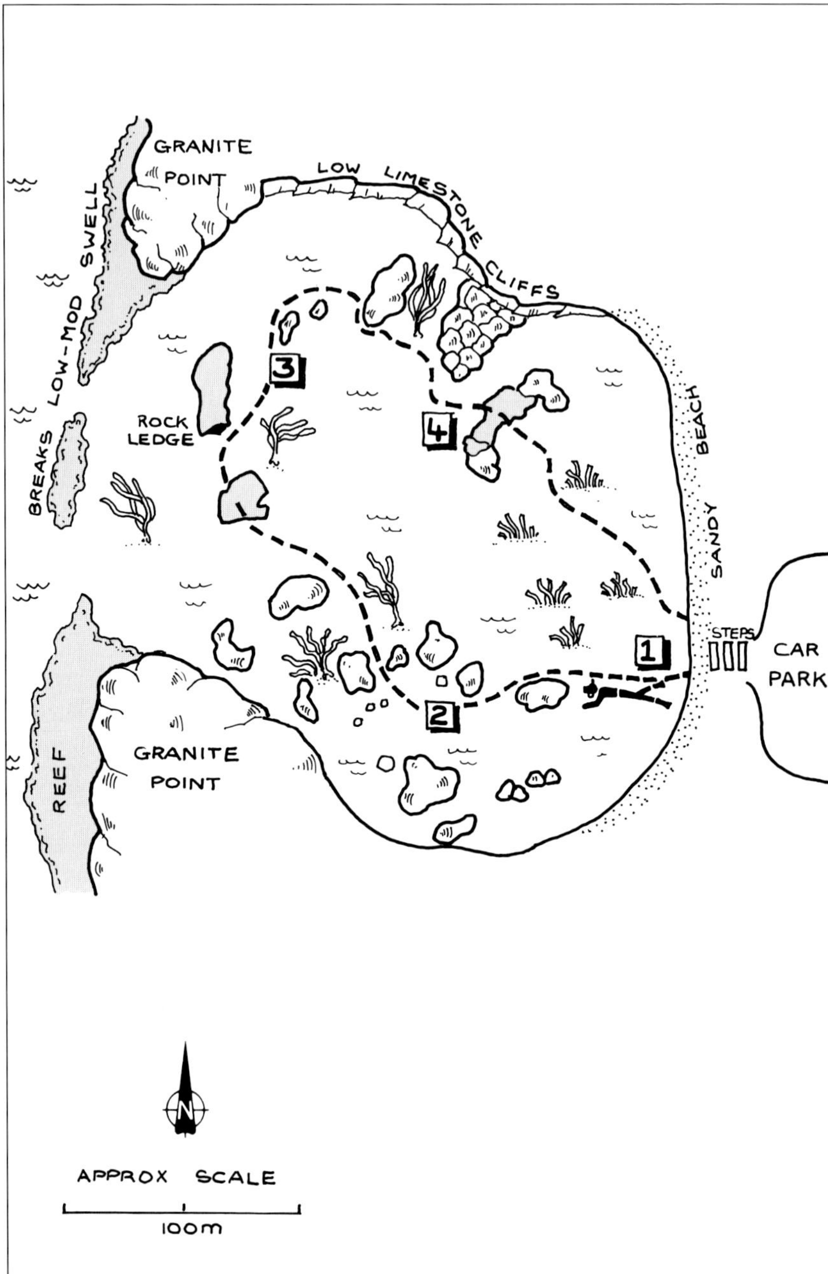
GRANITE POINT
LOW LIMESTONE CLIFFS
BREAKS LOW-MOD SWELL
ROCK LEDGE
3
4
SANDY BEACH
1
STEPS
CAR PARK
2
GRANITE POINT
REEF
N
APPROX SCALE
100m

Quarry Bay

16

How to get there: *Quarry Bay is little more than a kilometre north of the Leeuwin Lighthouse. The road is well signposted and ends at a gravel car park. Steps lead to the main beach, where there is easy access to the water's edge.*
Depth: *3-4 metres.*

Quarry Bay is a scenic 10 to 15 minute drive from the town of Augusta to the western side of one of the great capes in the world. Cape Leeuwin, where the Indian and Southern Oceans meet, is noted for its spectacular rugged scenery and cool temperate waters. The bay is open to the west and can be affected by prevailing ocean swells and south-westerly to north-westerly weather conditions. It is well sheltered, however, from the east, and the best diving conditions would be on a low to moderate swell with north-easterly to south-easterly winds. When the eastern side of the Cape is subject to unsuitable diving conditions, Quarry Bay can sometimes provide a pleasant sheltered alternative. It is best on snorkel because of the shallow depth. However, SCUBA can also be used as a personal choice.

1. Begin at the beach, near the steps. As you look seaward, the true beauty of this bay can be seen. Between the two rocky (granite) points at each end of the bay, a broken fringing reef can be seen occasionally breaking or awash under varying conditions. Towards the passage, small rounded granite boulders jut above the water 30 to 50 metres from shore. Swim towards them, across a shallow rocky seagrass bed, where small wrasse and sand whiting may be seen.
2. The jumble of small granites can be explored further seaward and towards the southern side of the bay. Still in relatively shallow water, seaweeds such as kelp and sargassum sway in the gentle surge. Circumnavigate the boulders and look under the low ledges and between narrow crevices, where scalyfins and bullseyes jealously guard their homes. Here, you might also be greeted by a small eagle ray.
3. Swim the bay in a clockwise direction, remaining inside the fringing reef entrance. As you cross open water towards the northern end of the bay, the depth increases to three or four metres. Amongst the rocky, weed-covered sea bed, small shoals of skippy and herring dash by, peering nervously at the diver. Zebra fish keep their distance near the bottom. Large submerged granite boulders, covered with seaweeds and sponges, are visible at this point. Ledges under the boulders disappear back into darkened caverns that become lighter as the eye adjusts, revealing western wirrah, moonlighter fish and buffalo bream.
4. As you follow the curve of the northern side of the bay back towards the beach, low limestone cliffs give way to a maze of granite boulders. These extend into

open seagrass beds, populated by king wrasse, dusky morwong and red-lipped morwong. A host of fish live amongst and beneath the rocks, including stripeys, western footballer sweep, butterflyfish and old wives. Return to the beach near the entry point.

Caution areas: *The swim should only be attempted during low to moderate swells. A slight current may be experienced under normal conditions, as the bay has only one opening for the inward and outward movement of water. Novice divers should remain within the confines of the bay, unless sea conditions are exceptionally calm.*
Degree of difficulty: *Easy to moderate, depending on conditions.*
Area's status: *Proposed marine park.*

Peter Lambert, Fran Stanley and Greg Pobar

COWRIES

Cowries are known for their highly polished shells, which usually have delightful colours and patterns. However, these otherwise alluring shellfish are generally encased in a fleshy camouflaging mantle, which covers most of the shell. Their distinctive shape disguises the fact that their shells are spirally coiled like other gastropod shells. Youngsters hardly resemble their parents and are seldom recognised as cowries, since their shells are long and thin, with a pointed spire. However, the last body whorl produced before the onset of maturity is swollen and covers the spire. The outer lip turns inwards, narrowing the opening to just a slit that extends for the length of the shell.

These animals do most of their feeding at night, browsing on small animals and plants that attach themselves to rock or coral. Females lay large egg masses of several hundred capsules, each capsule with 100 to 300 eggs. After hatching, the young usually go through a larval stage and will drift for a few days as plankton, before settling on the bottom. Cowries are highly prized by collectors, but those living within marine parks are protected and may not be removed.

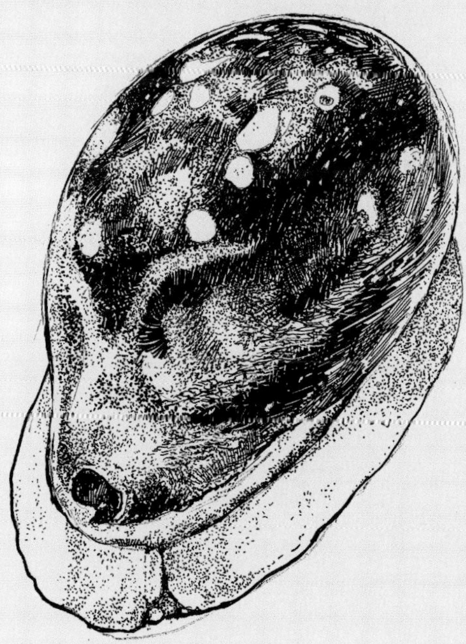

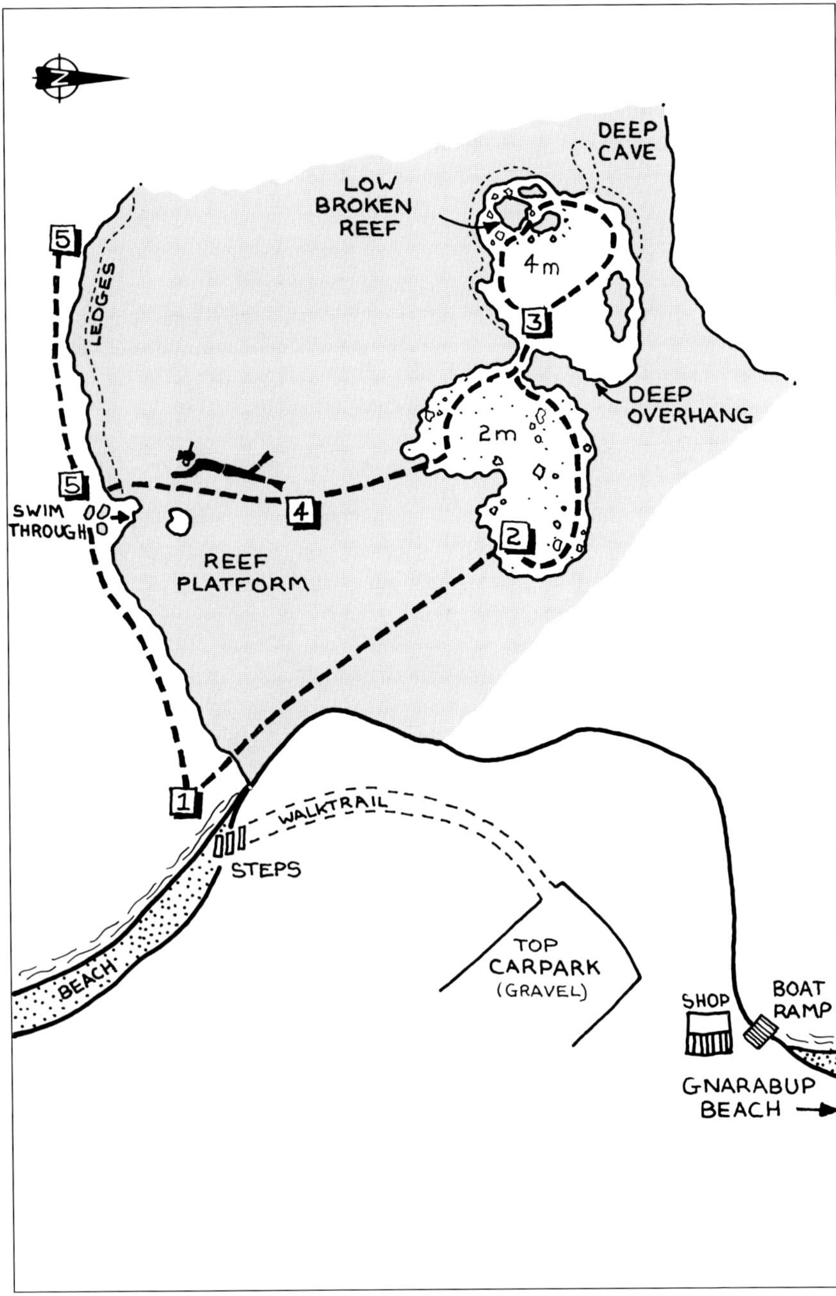

N
DEEP CAVE
LOW BROKEN REEF
4m
3
DEEP OVERHANG
5
LEDGES
2m
5
SWIM THROUGH
4
2
REEF PLATFORM
1
WALKTRAIL
STEPS
BEACH
TOP CARPARK (GRAVEL)
SHOP
BOAT RAMP
GNARABUP BEACH

South of Gnarabup Beach

17

How to get there: *Swim from shore.*
Depth: *2-4 metres.*

Two large and inviting holes in the reef platform south of Gnarabup Beach can be explored either on snorkel or SCUBA. However, the entry point is a 150 metre walk from the top car park at Gnarabup Beach, so your desire to dive the area on SCUBA may be limited by your readiness to carry gear for this distance. However, it is worth the effort.

1. Follow the track that leads from the north-western corner of the gravel car park to the steps. Make your way across the reef platform to the first hole, which is about 30 metres from shore.
2. This hole is only around two metres deep, and it has numerous ledges and overhangs around its edge, while rubble and shell debris litter the sandy floor. Sea hares are plentiful at certain times of the year on the reef top around the rim. These greenish-brown, slug-like creatures are well camouflaged amongst the green and brown seaweed on which they feed. Unlike true sea slugs, they have a small thin horny shell that is partly or completely covered by their mantle. The animals derive their name from the two pairs of large fleshy tentacles that protrude from the head. Each of these has an unusual fold that resembles a rabbit's ear. Sea hares have an interesting life history and die after laying their eggs, when their dead or dying bodies are often washed ashore. Fish species include banded sweep, dusky morwong, moonlighters (including juveniles with the diagnostic spot on the dorsal and anal fins), wrasse, tarwhine, buffalo bream and skipjack trevally.
3. A narrow gap leads to another large hole a little further from shore, which contains zebra fish in huge numbers. This is about four metres deep and would be best appreciated on SCUBA. The westernmost section has a small, but deep, cave and a patch of low, broken reef about two metres high, which conceals hidden passages and caverns.
4. As you swim to the southern edge of the reef, watch out for the interesting animals that inhabit the shallow reef platform. There are many reasonably large trumpet and turban shells nestling in nooks and crannies, while you may also spot an octopus secreted in a crevice.

5. On the far southern edge of the reef platform there is a deep ledge and swimthrough, although it is not advisable to enter it if you are snorkelling. However, take some time to explore the ledges that undercut the reef, before you make your way back to the beach.

Caution areas: *Swimming into caverns and under ledges can be hazardous.*
Degree of difficulty: *Easy in good conditions.*
Area's status: *The waters are proposed for reservation as a marine park.*

John Edwards, Carolyn Thomson-Dans and Peter Dans

HMAS SWAN

The largest scuttled ship in the southern hemisphere now lies in Geographe Bay, near Dunsborough, after a former navy warship was sunk there on December 14, 1997 to provide the diving experience of a lifetime.

The 2 750 tonne *HMAS Swan* was launched in 1967 and carried 200 crew. She is more than 140 metres long and now lies in 30 metres of clear water, protected by Cape Naturaliste. The navigation and antennae tower is about eight metres below the surface, with the upper deck at about 15 metres. A "no fishing" area has been designated for 500 metres around the ship, to provide a haven for the area's abundant sea life.

The Geographe Bay Artificial Reef Society cleaned the *HMAS Swan* thoroughly before it was sunk to prevent oil, silt or debris hampering divers, and more than 10 000 spectators lined the shores or watched from boats when she was scuttled.

A permit is required for privately owned and commercial boats to take divers to the scuttled ship. The best way to see the *HMAS Swan* is by means of a dive charter. Local dive shops offer charters to see the outside of the ship, while an Advanced Wreck Dive Course can be completed to enable more experienced divers to explore inside the ship.

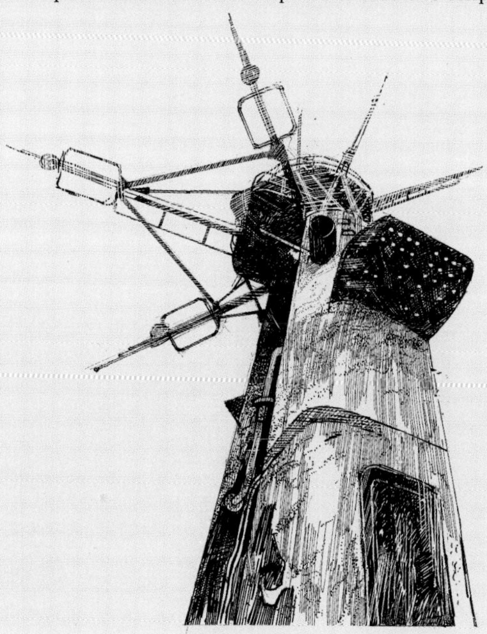

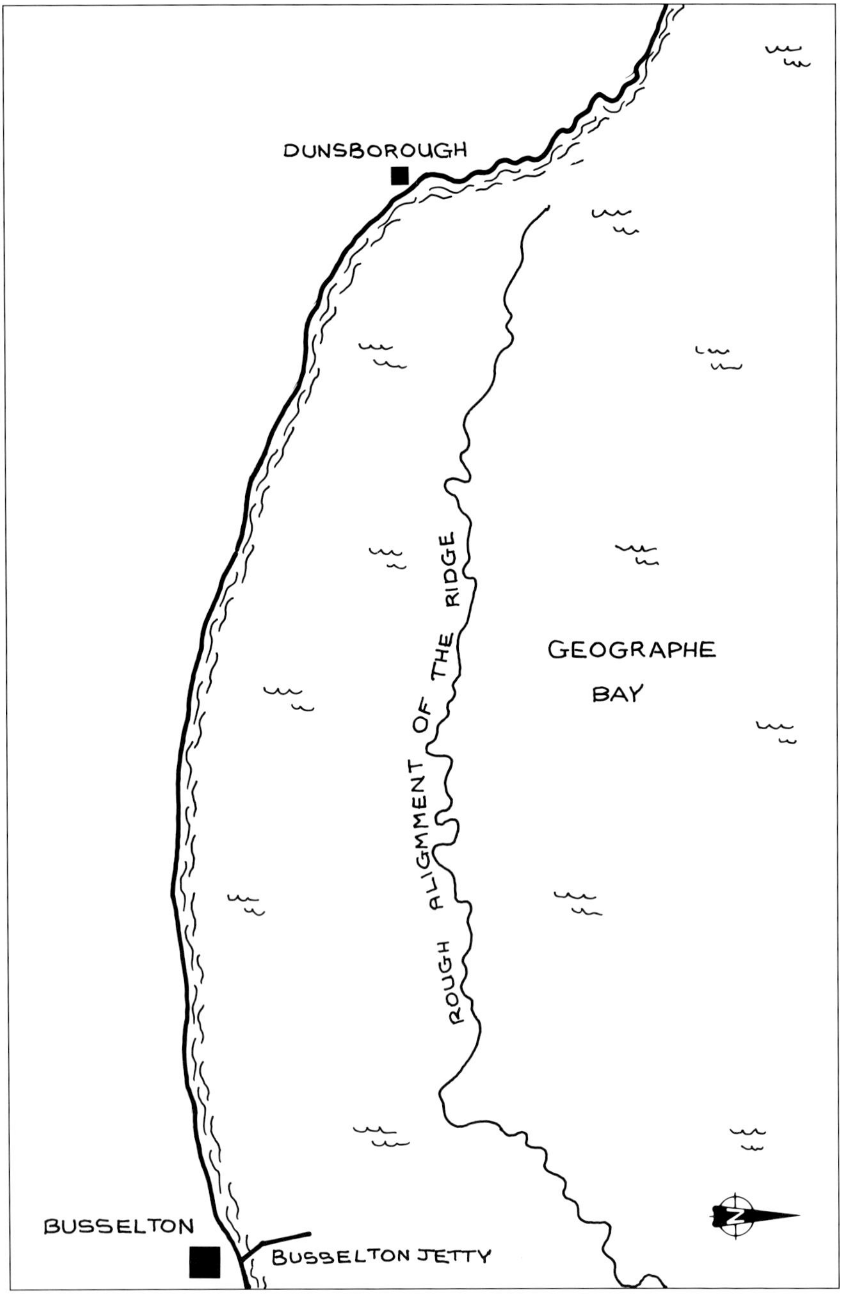
DUNSBOROUGH
ROUGH ALIGNMENT OF THE RIDGE
GEOGRAPHE BAY
BUSSELTON
BUSSELTON JETTY

Geographe Bay Ridge

18

How to get there: *By boat with an echo sounder from Busselton or Dunsborough.*
Depth: *16-18 metres.*

The Geographe Bay Ridge is a low reef that follows the coast from north of Dunsborough to past Peppermint Beach, north-east of Busselton. Its distance from shore varies from around four kilometres out from Dunsborough, to about seven kilometres from Busselton. The ridge roughly coincides with the 15 metre contour on the marine chart DMH 451. To find the ridge, you must pay close attention to the echo sounder. Head straight out from the shore, and watch carefully until you run over a narrow band that comes up to about 16 metres from a flat bottom of 18 metres. Chances are, it will be the ridge. However, the ridge is sometimes hard to find, as it is interrupted with low patches that don't register on the echo sounder. Don't persist too far out in 20 metres of water; turn back towards the shore and move either west or east slightly. Persistence usually ends in a magnificent dive.

The limestone reef generally rises from a flat bottom of 18 metres to 16 metres, although in one area west of Busselton, it rises up to around 12 metres. Here, larger bombies tower above the usual low ledges that pocket the ridge. In a few areas closer to Dunsborough, the ridge divides and becomes two ridges, 20 metres or so apart.

This ridge appears to be an important habitat for many of the fish found in Geographe Bay. Thousands of juvenile fish live under the ledges, and among the most prolific seagrasses that grow on the reef. They include young truncate coralfish, old wives, bullseyes, cardinalfish, leatherjackets and wrasse. Many wonderfully-shaped sponges and some hard corals also grow on top of the reef, while small gorgonian fan corals and soft corals are sometimes found under the ledges. There are also giant cuttlefish, stingrays (including very large bull rays and eagle rays), six-banded sea perches that often sit in cup sponges, harlequin fish, Western Australian jewfish, samson fish, wobbegong sharks and, if you are lucky, a knight fish. This fish looks a little like a pineapple with two luminescent spots on its lower jaw. These spots are reddish-orange by day, but fluoresce a bluish-green at night. The knight fish usually hides under the limestone ledges of the ridge.

Caution areas: *Watch the weather. If it starts to come up, head back to shore.*
Degree of difficulty: *Moderate to difficult.*
Area's status: *Geographe Bay is a proposed marine reserve.*

Ann Storrie and Brian Cleaver

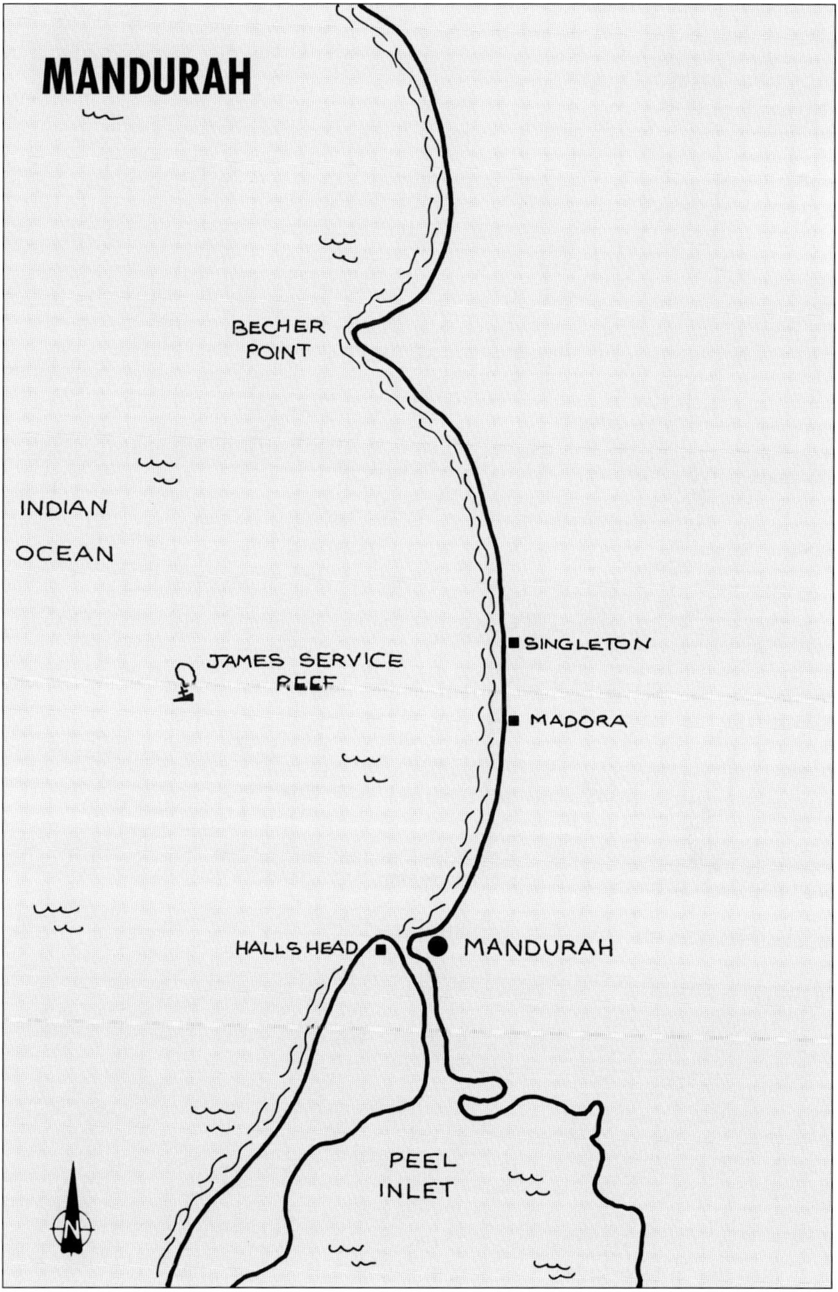
MANDURAH
BECHER POINT
INDIAN OCEAN
JAMES SERVICE REEF
SINGLETON
MADORA
HALLS HEAD
MANDURAH
PEEL INLET
N

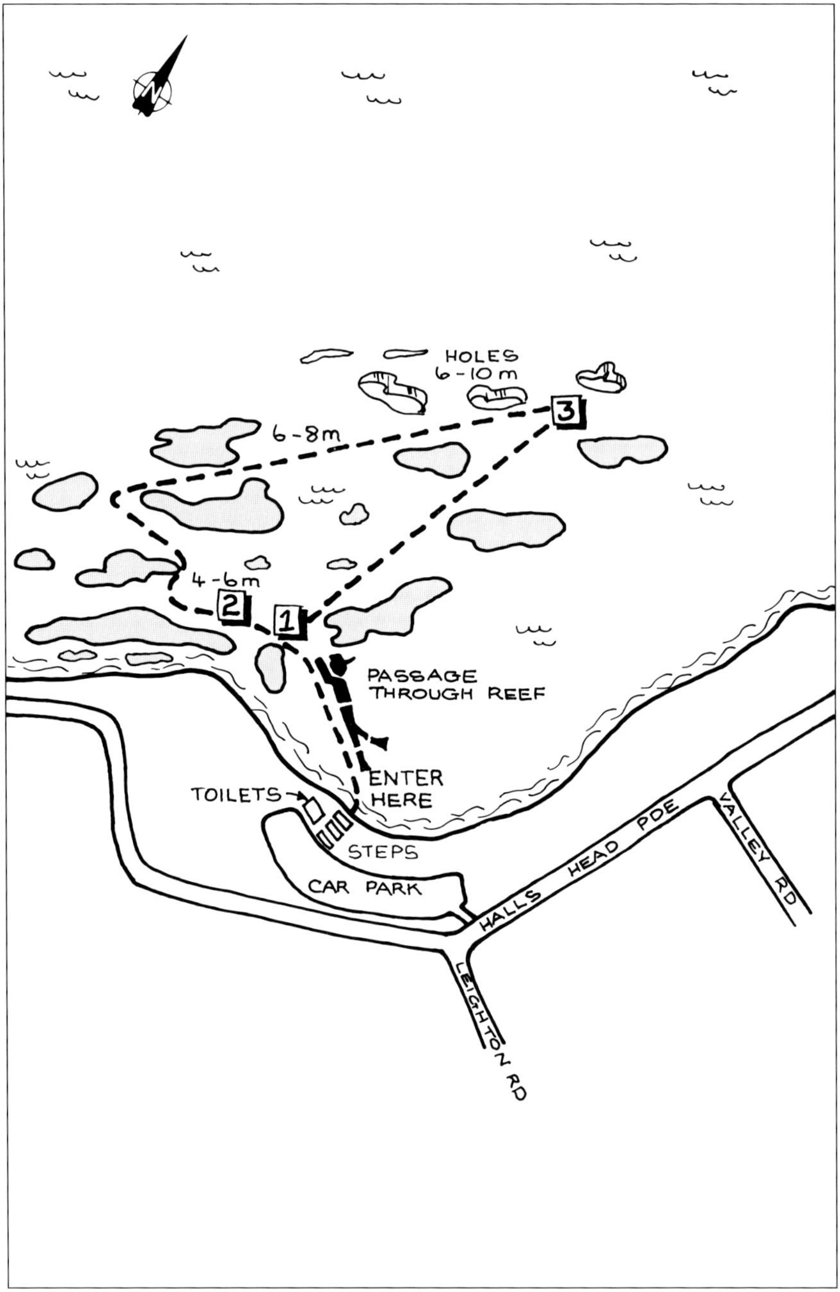
N
HOLES
6-10m
6-8m
4-6m
2
1
3
PASSAGE
THROUGH REEF
ENTER
HERE
TOILETS
STEPS
CAR PARK
HALLS HEAD PDE
VALLEY RD
LEIGHTON RD

Blue Bay, Halls Head

19

How to get there: *Swim from the beach.*
Depth: *5-10 metres.*

Blue Bay is a popular dive location for all the family. Whilst this site is more exposed to the prevailing south-westerly winds than nearby Roberts Point, which is about 800 metres north, it is often dived first thing in the morning when offshore breezes are consistent. Blue Bay is also a popular location for surfers, so if any swell exists it is suggested that you relocate to another site, as it is prone to poor visibility and can be unpleasant when the swell is running. The site has a good-sized car park, toilets, shower and a grassed area for kitting up. A shop and telephone booth are available about 400 metres east along Valley Road if required. There is a flight of stairs that is relatively steep and may cause some discomfort when you exit the beach with SCUBA equipment.

1. From the beach, swim towards the gap between the two reef platforms, approximately 60 metres from shore.
2. Proceed around the circuit in a clockwise direction. Immediately to your left, you will notice some overhangs and shallow caves in about five metres of water. These are rich in marine life, including buffalo bream, banded sweep and a variety of rock cod. The defensive western scalyfin can also be seen. This fish is very territorial and will protect its domain by swimming repeatedly and rapidly past the inquisitive and intrusive diver. Soft corals, sponges and sea squirts line the walls, as do species of sea star and crustaceans.
3. Continue around until you reach the most northern extremity of the dive in this area, where deeper holes to 10 metres can be found. Occasionally these holes attract resting mulloway and dusky morwongs, large fish that predate in the evenings. These holes provide keen photographers with the opportunity to photograph a variety of fish species in clean water.

Caution areas: *Keep clear of boat traffic and always tow a dive flag. Never dive on moderate to strong sea breezes and avoid days with a moderate to heavy swell.*
Degree of difficulty: *Easy to moderate, depending on conditions.*

Matthew and Alan Byrne, with assistance from the Mandurah Dive Academy

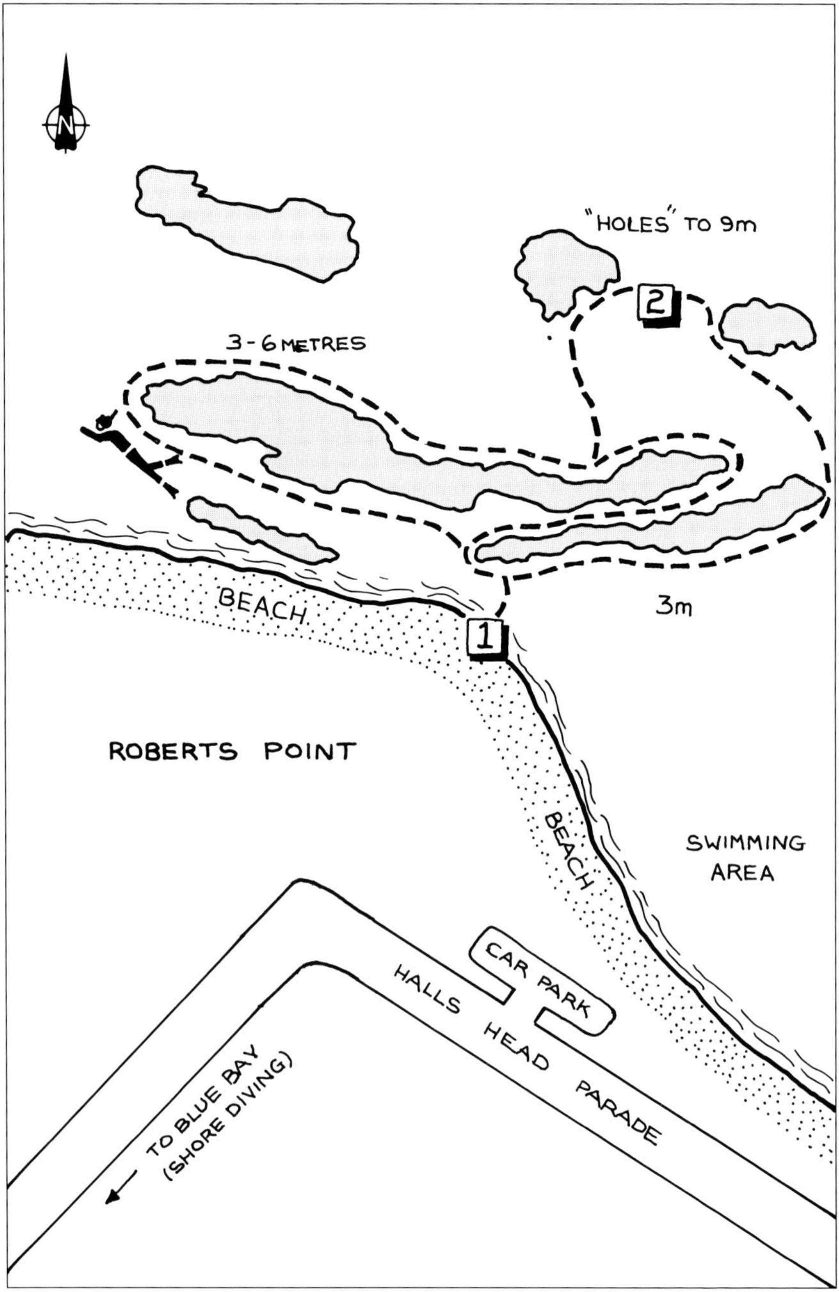
N
"HOLES" TO 9m
2
3-6 METRES
BEACH
1
3m
ROBERTS POINT
BEACH
SWIMMING
AREA
CAR PARK
HALLS HEAD PARADE
TO BLUE BAY
(SHORE DIVING)

Roberts Point, Halls Head

How to get there: *Park in the most westerly car park and walk 60 metres to the point.*
Depth: *3-9 metres.*

Roberts Point, at Halls Head, is a popular swimming location for all the family. Just west of the beach, known locally as Doddi's Bay, the site is popular with snorkellers and SCUBA divers during the summer holiday period, as it is protected from prevailing southerly winds and offers comfortable beach picnicking on shore. Like most shore dives, visibility is greatly affected by swell, so it should be avoided in moderate to strong sea breezes. To reach the location, drive over the Old Traffic Bridge, then veer right over the Port Mandurah Canals Bridge onto Mary Street. Follow Mary Street around past the Mandurah Yacht Club, past the shops on the left and park in the most westerly car park, which has a display of anchors and information on the Mandurah Wreck Trail. There is a large grassed area to kit up and toilets, shops, barbecue facilities and public telephones are close by.

1. From the entry point, head in a northerly direction. The first group of platform reefs can be found in shallow water about three metres deep. This first group is typical of the limestone reef system found in local waters. They are heavily encrusted with bull kelp (*Ecklonia radiata*) and, in some cases, abalone. Schools of buffalo bream, banded sweep, herring and tailor can also be found. The reef system has numerous tight holes and overhangs, where western rock lobster can also be found. A closer look under the overhangs will reveal a colourful yellow and orange animal commonly known as Ellis's sea fan. This fragile soft coral should not be touched, as it is easily damaged.
2. After leaving this cluster of reefs, divers should proceed with caution to the north. This site is somewhat deeper, with holes to nine metres. Similar species can be found at this location, however, other species such as wrasse and boxfish can be seen in and around these holes.

Caution areas: *Keep clear of boat traffic, never dive on days with moderate to strong sea breezes and avoid days with moderate to heavy swell.*
Degree of difficulty: *Easy to moderate, depending on conditions.*

Alan Byrne, with assistance from Mandurah Dive Academy

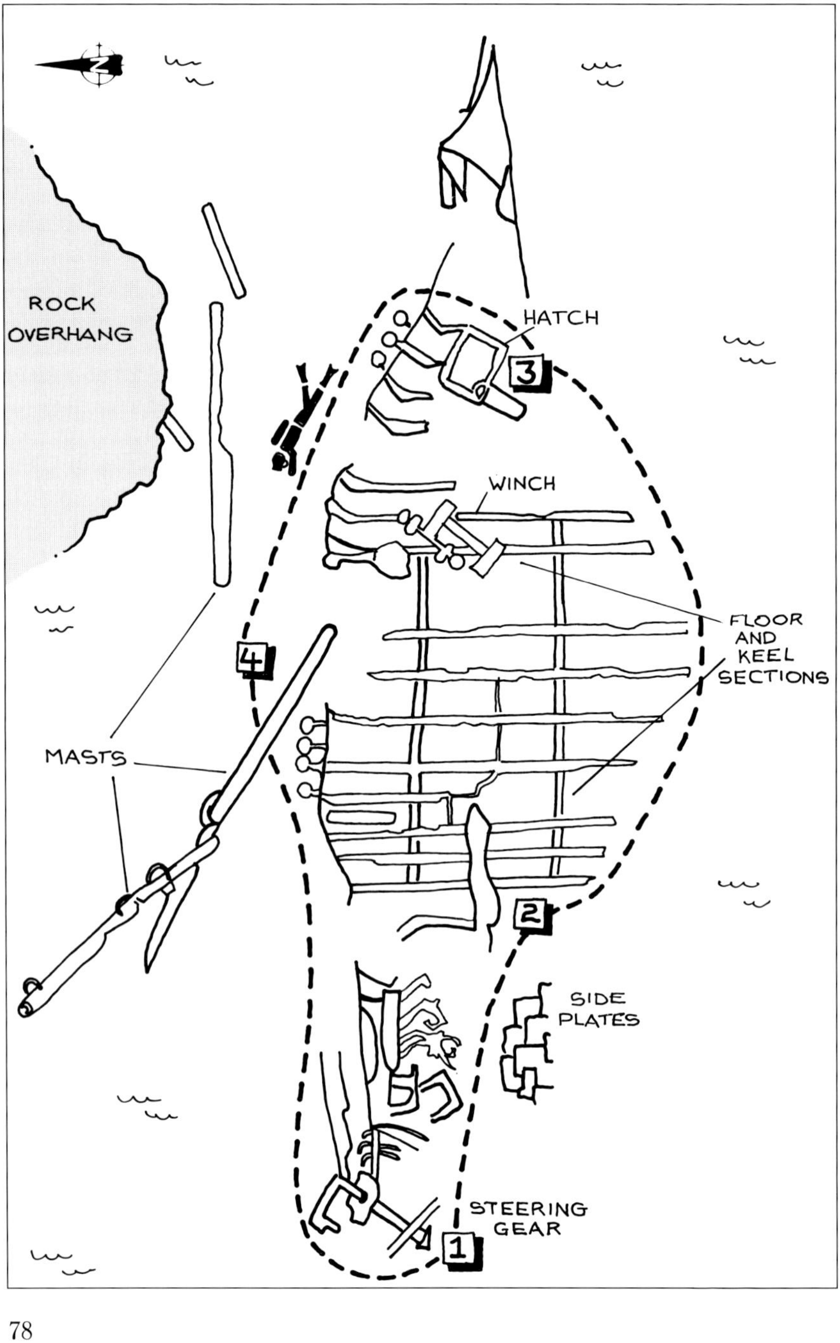
ROCK
OVERHANG
HATCH
3
WINCH
FLOOR
AND
KEEL
SECTIONS
4
MASTS
2
SIDE
PLATES
STEERING
GEAR
1

The wreck of the *James Service* 21

How to get there: *By boat from Mandurah or Rockingham.*
Depth: *3-8 metres.*

On July 23, 1878, a local stockman noticed the masts of a ship submerged in offshore waters, just west of the mouth of the Murray River, but it was too rough to send a rescue boat to assist people seen clinging to the rigging. A longboat marked with the words "James Service, Melbourne" was located on the beach nearby. The next day, cases, tins of castor oil, luggage, cabin fittings and pieces of deck began to wash ashore. Then the body of a woman with the name "J Towers" stitched onto her petticoat and drawers was found. Over the next few days, several other bodies were found along the coast. A fully clothed body in officer's dress was believed to be the mate, Mr Foreman.

The *James Service*, a 440 ton iron barque with three masts, was en route from Calcutta to Melbourne. In Penang it picked up members of a theatrical group on their way to Melbourne. The ship also carried 3 000 cases of castor oil, 1 000 bales of sack bags and 600 bales of jute, and was on a course that should have taken it several hundred miles from the coast. None of the 10 passengers and 10 crew members survived, but it is thought that the *James Service* was wrecked in rough seas on the night of July 22, possibly as it headed to Fremantle for emergency repairs. A diary washed ashore recorded that the vessel had encountered extremely rough seas for some time.

The wreck of the *James Service* is one of the most popular dives in the Mandurah area. It lies on the southern end of the Murray Reef, about 4.5 nautical miles offshore, on a bearing 331° north-west of the entrance of the Mandurah Estuary. When approaching the reef, do so with extreme caution - even on a calm day the reef is not always visible and is only one metre from the surface. The Department of Transport has placed a marker on the reef at latitude 32° 27.98 south and longitude 115° 39.51 east. The wreck is about 140 metres due north of the marker (the marker has broken free during extreme weather conditions, so this distance may not be entirely accurate). It is advisable to anchor a good distance from the reef, paying careful attention to prevailing and predicted winds.

1. The vessel lies in an east-west direction, with the steering, mast pieces, ribs and underlying frames all visible, and the structure rises two and a half metres from the bottom. Commence your dive from the most western end. Upon your descent,

you will notice the steering gear, which at first glance looks like a medium-sized anchor. Like all the remaining wreckage, the steering gear is heavily encrusted with marine life.

2. After swimming east for a further 25 to 30 metres, you can see large planks forming a grid spanning 40 metres wide and 50 metres long. This is the floor and keel section, the end of which is unmistakably marked by a large winch.
3. The final section is marked by a large steel frame about 10 metres by 10 metres. This was apparently the hatch frame.
4. The masts can be seen a few metres north of the floor and keel section, between the main wreck and a large rock overhang. If you look closely, some of the rigging gear can be seen on the masts. The site has good visibility on a low swell, sometimes up to 25 metres. The marine life is plentiful, with schools of stripeys and wrasse accompanying you on your dive.

Caution areas: *The wreck is in an exposed position, so do not dive it in rough conditions or when there is strong surge.*
Degree of difficulty: *Moderate to difficult, depending on conditions.*
Area's status: *The* James Service *is a protected wreck site and artefacts can't be removed from the area.*

Alan Byrne, with assistance from the Mandurah Dive Academy

SEAHORSES

Despite its bizarre appearance, the seahorse is a fish. Western Australia has its very own species of seahorse, found in sheltered bays between Augusta and Shark Bay. These delightful animals inhabit areas that are reasonably protected, such as reefs, seagrass meadows and jetties. Individuals are often washed ashore during storms and subsequently found dead on beaches.

These curled pipefish were described in ancient times as part fish and part horse. Seahorses have an elongated snout, a tail that can be used to grasp objects and bodies which are encased in bony segments.

Their mating practices are as unusual as their appearance. The female lays her eggs directly into the male's pouch, where he will fertilise and incubate them until they hatch. They will then emerge as fully developed, miniature seahorses from a small hole in the pouch.

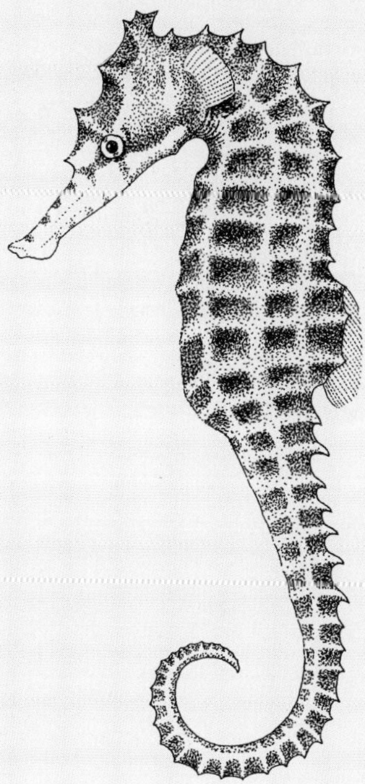

SHOALWATER ISLANDS MARINE PARK

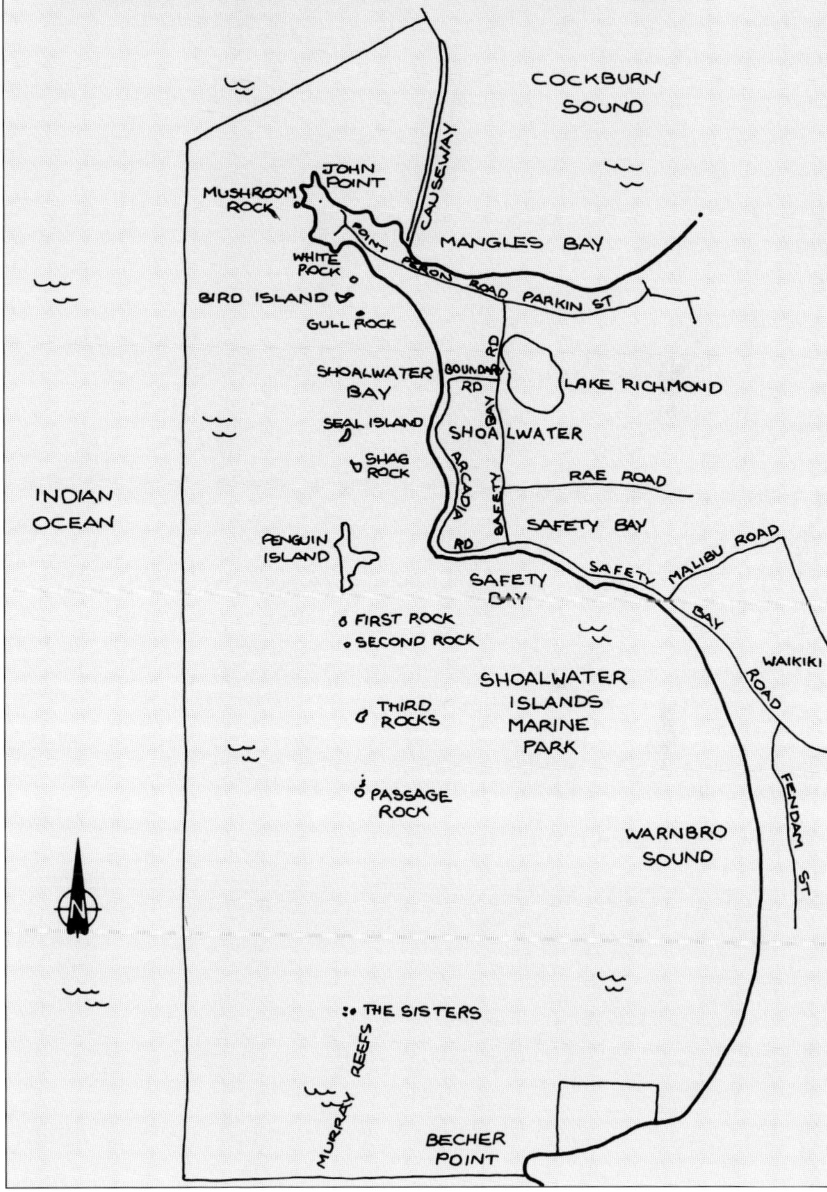

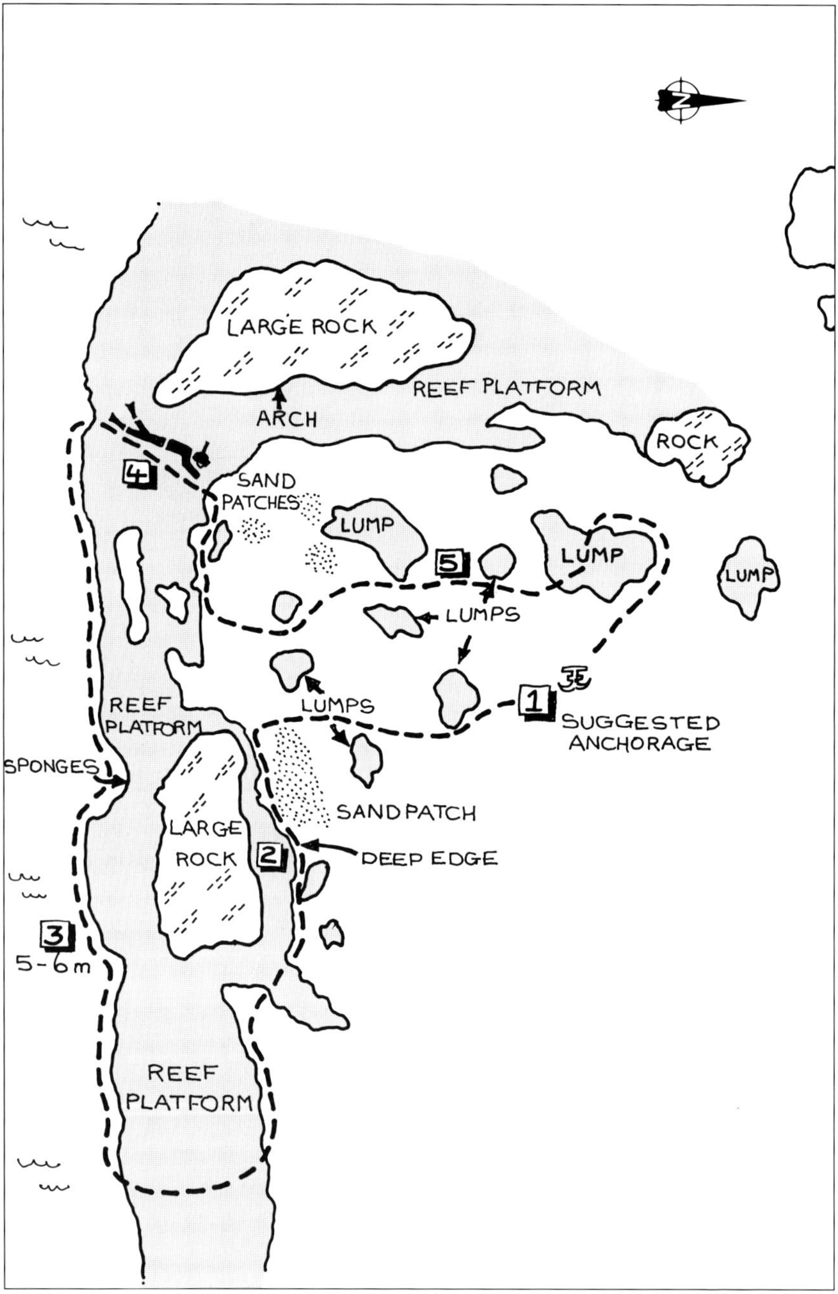
LARGE ROCK
REEF PLATFORM
ARCH
ROCK
4
SAND PATCHES
LUMP
5
LUMP
LUMP
LUMPS
1
SUGGESTED ANCHORAGE
LUMPS
REEF PLATFORM
SPONGES
SAND PATCH
LARGE ROCK
2
DEEP EDGE
3
5-6m
REEF PLATFORM

The Sisters

22

How to get there: *By boat from Rockingham or Safety Bay. Please check the weather conditions before leaving, as the return trip can be hazardous in a small boat if the weather comes up.*
Depth: *2-6 metres.*

The Sisters are a series of limestone reefs at the southern end of the Shoalwater Islands Marine Park. They are easy to find using the Warnbro Chart, as they are marked by a group of rocks protruding above the surface, and offer snorkellers and SCUBA divers an excellent opportunity to experience an area rich in marine life.

1. Begin on the north-eastern side of the two largest rocks that make up The Sisters, and proceed in a clockwise direction.
2. The reef walls, and the walls of the crevices and caves, are coated with soft and hard corals, anemones, sponges, ascidians, gorgonian fan corals and sea stars. Sea cucumbers, nudibranchs and bryozoans are scattered over various underwater surfaces, while crayfish and shelled molluscs hide under ledges and in caves.
3. The deepest area is on the southern side of the reef platform. However, the surge is often very strong here, so if you are snorkelling be watchful and also take care not to venture too near the reef's sharp edges. Clouds of baitfish, large schools of buffalo bream and schools of herring can be seen on this side of The Sisters.
4. Return to your boat via the numerous channels or over the reef between the two largest rocks that form The Sisters. Large schools of fish cruise the reef. Scalyfin, banded sweep and old wives are common reef dwellers, as are various wrasse and gobies. Some red-lipped morwongs can also be seen hiding in crevices. A King George whiting may be seen lurking surreptitiously near the reef, blending into the sand below, ready to ambush its latest meal.
5. Areas of high broken reef surround the reef platform. Thick beds of kelp cover most of the high broken reef, and seagrasses colonise the sandy floor. The kelp beds hide abundant growths of coralline and turf algae, as well as patchy distributions of sponges, ascidians and snails. On some lumps, you may be able to see small patches of brown honeycomb coral, which is similar to brain coral.

Caution areas: *The reef's southern side is subject to strong surge, so take care.*
Degree of difficulty: *Easy to moderate, depending on conditions.*
Area's status: *Lies within the Shoalwater Islands Marine Park.*

Brad Daw, Carolyn Thomson-Dans, Peter Dans and Terry Goodlich

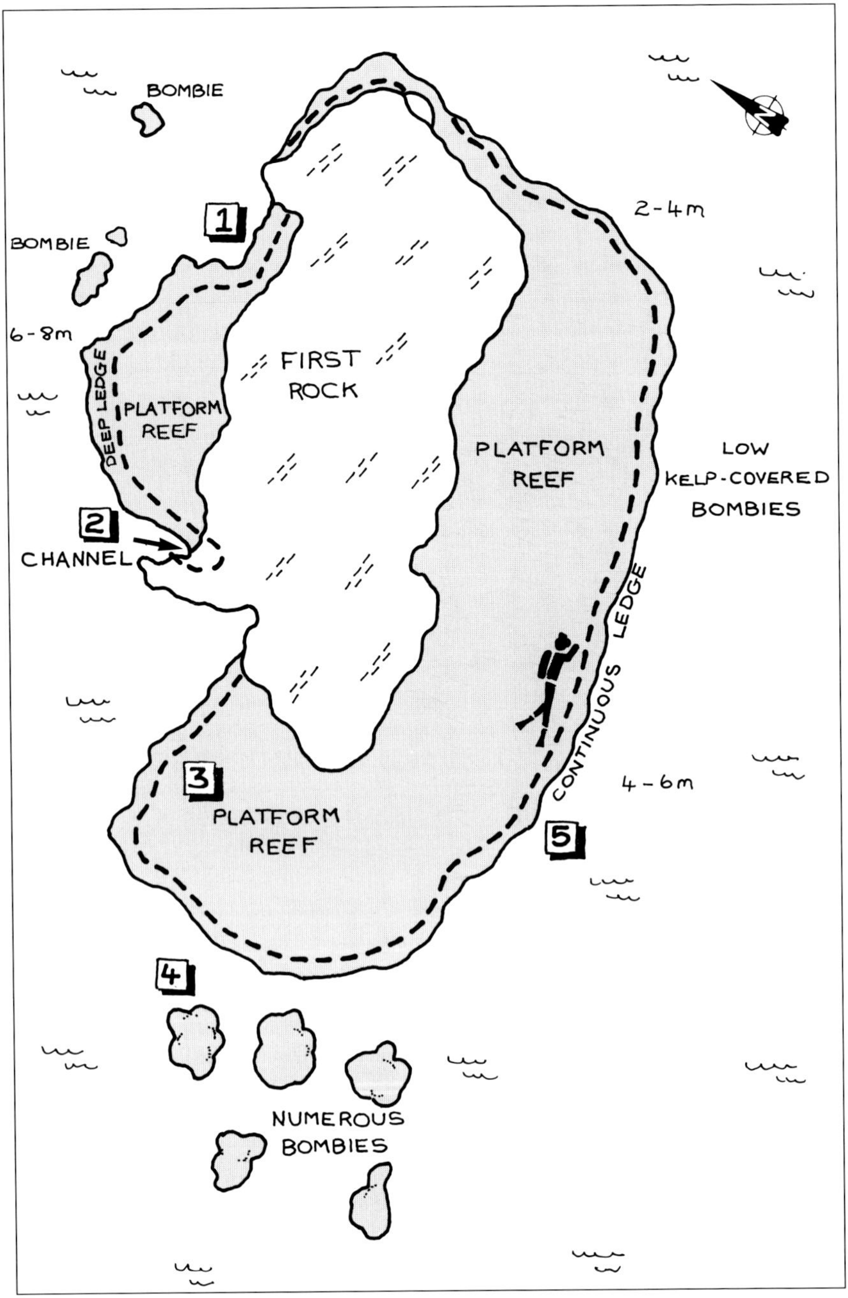
BOMBIE
BOMBIE
1
2-4m
6-8m
DEEP LEDGE
PLATFORM REEF
FIRST ROCK
PLATFORM REEF
LOW KELP-COVERED BOMBIES
2
CHANNEL
CONTINUOUS LEDGE
3
PLATFORM REEF
4-6m
5
4
NUMEROUS BOMBIES

First Rock

23

How to get there: *By boat from Rockingham or Safety Bay.*
Depth: *2-5 metres.*

First Rock is the first large rock to the south of Penguin Island. For full appreciation of its beauty, this dive site demands exploration by SCUBA. However, it is definitely a good weather dive. Cave networks extend right under First Rock, and winds over 10 kilometres and a swell over one metre can make conditions dangerous.

1. Deep and spectacular ledges undercut the platform reef on the western side of the rock. They are inhabited by schools of huge buffalo bream.
2. Continue to follow the ledge south. In the broken ground, wobbegongs are tucked tightly under ledges. A cave can be found where the reef platform terminates just before a protruding section of the islet. Some interesting small patches of a brown coral inhabit the ledge near the cave.
3. A short distance onwards, the reef platform commences again. Anemones, sea stars and shellfish such as abalone live on top of the platform. If you keep a careful eye open you may spot an octopus, lurking in the weed and crevices. If you swim over the top of the reef, you may startle a number of large buffalo bream. These fish graze on the algae (seaweeds) which grow on the reef top.
4. Numerous high, kelp-covered bombies lie to the west of the reef platform.
5. The ledge continues virtually all the way around the reef edge. However, the depth is considerably shallower on the south-eastern side of the rock (only about two metres) and the ledge is therefore far less spectacular.

Caution areas: *The western side of the rock is fairly exposed and should be avoided if there is a strong surge or winds of more than 10 km/hour.*
Degree of difficulty: *Moderate to difficult, depending on conditions.*
Area's status: *Lies within the Shoalwater Islands Marine Park.*

Carolyn Thomson-Dans, Brad Daw and Terry Goodlich

CARNAC ISLAND TO THE STRAGGLERS

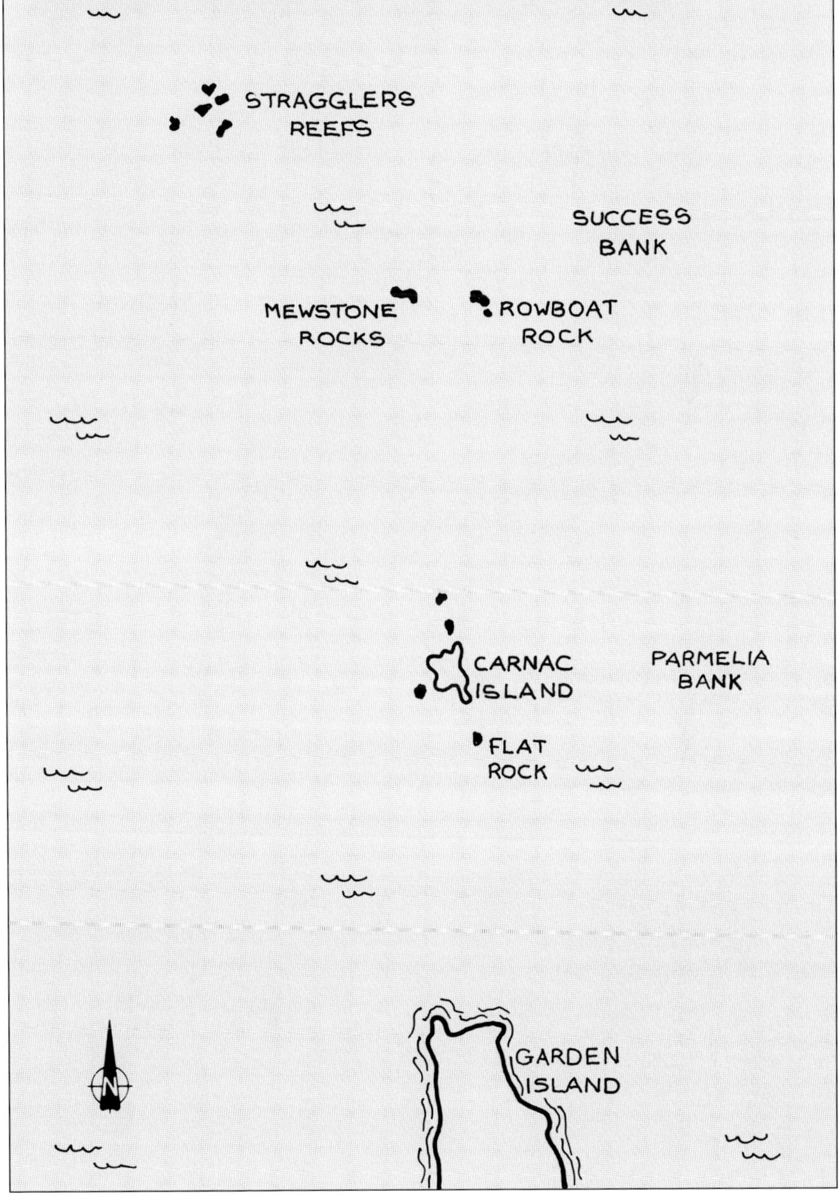

CARNAC ISLAND
FLAT ROCK
3
2
1
4 m
APPROX SCALE
N

Carnac Island - east of Flat Rock

24

How to get there: *By boat from Fremantle.*
Depth: *1-4 metres.*

This site is recommended for novice snorkellers and people who enjoy fossicking.

1. Begin at the southern end of Flat Rock. The reef has some extremely picturesque swimthroughs and caves in about four metres. Schools of buffalo bream, crested morwong, juvenile white-barred boxfish, herring, scalyfin and numerous wrasse inhabit the area. Sea squirts, sea tulips, sponges and other invertebrates nestle in the waving fronds that cover the reefs. This area is subject to surge, so take care. Some of the small lumps are greatly undercut, and crammed with masses of colourful gorgonians, schools of juvenile bullseyes and other creatures.
2. Though less interesting country, the reefs along the south-eastern part of the rock may reveal well-camouflaged octopuses among seaweeds, rocks or in crevices. You may even be joined by an inquisitive sea lion, but you should always remember that they are wild animals and can be unpredictable. Never approach a sea lion (instead allow them to approach you if they wish) or attempt to touch them. Keep your hands close to your body and your movements to a minimum, to avoid startling the animal. If a sea lion becomes overly playful or aggressive (such as nipping at flippers or nudging your body), you should move away slowly and leave the water.
3. A drift snorkel over the shallow reef top will prove to be a fossicker's delight. Thousands of green and red anemones vie for space on the reef top. The green ones are the reef anemone and the red species is the cherry anemone. This flower-like animal withdraws its tentacles into the body column when the tide is low, resembling a cherry. Astute observers can see false Tasmanian blennies peeping from holes in the shallow reef top. These cheeky fish can be recognised by the yellow tentacles above their eyes.

Caution areas: *Watch out for surge on the southern end and take care when swimming under ledges and into caverns. Be cautious around sea lions.*
Degree of difficulty: *Easy.*
Area's status: *Nearby Carnac Island is a nature reserve. The waters surrounding the island have been proposed for consideration as a marine park.*

John Edwards, Carolyn Thomson-Dans and Stephanie Crawford

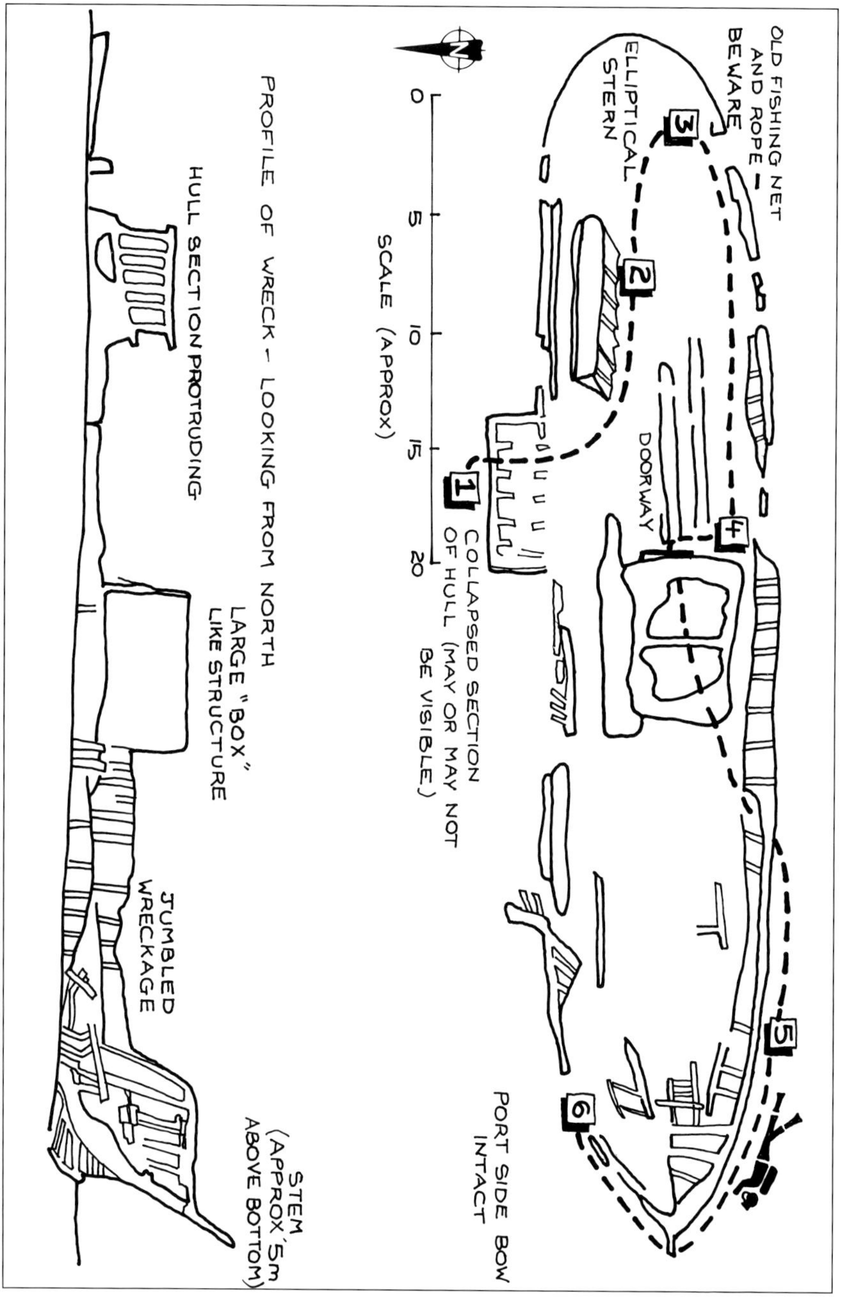
OLD FISHING NET AND ROPE – BEWARE
ELLIPTICAL STERN
N
0
5
10
15
20
SCALE (APPROX)
DOORWAY
COLLAPSED SECTION OF HULL (MAY OR MAY NOT BE VISIBLE)
PORT SIDE BOW INTACT
1
2
3
4
5
6
PROFILE OF WRECK – LOOKING FROM NORTH
HULL SECTION PROTRUDING
LARGE "BOX" LIKE STRUCTURE
JUMBLED WRECKAGE
STEM (APPROX 5m ABOVE BOTTOM)

The dredge west of the Stragglers 25

How to get there: *By boat from Fremantle or Cockburn.*
Depth: *22 metres maximum.*

An old steel dredge, thought to be either the *Fremantle* or the *Governor*, was discovered in January 1998, 3 km west of the Stragglers Rocks. The *Fremantle*, a bucket dredge 45 metres long, was used in the early 1900s to dig Fremantle Harbour and was scuttled in 1936. The *Governor* is supposed to have been scuttled south-east of Cape Vlamingh, but its length of 53.34 metres accords more closely with the length of the Stragglers wreck. This recently discovered wreck is one of the most interesting and attractive dives in the Perth area. Much of the superstructure is still visible. It lies on a sandy bottom in 22 metres of water. The wreck is more than 50 metres long, and the port side is fairly intact, with the deck beams lying inside the hull. The swell can be quite strong, but is ideal on calm balmy days. However, due to its depth and degree of difficulty, it is a site for qualified advanced divers only.

The wreck is at latitude 32° 03.486 south, longitude 115° 36.102 east, bearing 100° from the Stragglers and 312° from the lighthouse on Rottnest. When on the co-ordinates according to your GPS, drop a weight attached by light line to a small float and do a circular search with the echo sounder on. Any visible "needle" will be the wreck. It should be within 100 to 150 metres of your marker float.

1. The wreck is completely surrounded by sand. If you approach from the north, you may or may not be able to see (depending on whether or not it is covered with sand) a collapsed section of hull that resembles a grate.
2. A large section of hull protrudes above the wreckage. Large fronds of white polyps of a soft coral (*Carijoa multiflora*) can be seen on the hull, and colourful sponges grow in strange shapes out from the sides. Beautiful orange, yellow and red gorgonians, plus all types of ascidians form part of the mass of colour on the outside, while yellow zoanthids, often hidden in their pink matrix, coat the inside and other protected areas of the wreck.
3. If you investigate the stern, beware of some old fishing net and rope that has become entangled in the wreckage.
4. In the middle of the wreck is a large "box"-like structure, about the size of a small room. You can actually go in through the door and swim out through the top. Bullseyes hang around the north-western corner of this structure. Fish are more

abundant on this wreck than at most other dive sites around Perth, possibly because it has lain undisturbed for so many years. There is also little reef in the vicinity, hence the marine life congregates around the steel structure. Stingarees, immature jewfish, harlequin fish, scorpionfish, old wives, bullseyes, wrasse, scalyfins and many more species have made the wreck their home. You may even find an enormous baler shell among the wreckage.

5. Towards the bow, there is a massive encrusted wall facing south-west.
6. The bow rises to within seven metres of the surface and is covered with sponges, soft corals, gorgonians and ascidians. In fact, the invertebrate life is as prolific as anywhere around Rottnest. This is one of the best spots on the wreck and the antler sponges on the port side are exceptionally beautiful.

Caution areas: *Beware of old fishing nets and rope entangled in the wreckage. Wait for optimum conditions and do not dive the site in a strong swell.*
Degree of difficulty: *Difficult. A site for qualified advanced divers only.*

Mike Lapwood, Ann Storrie and Brad Daw

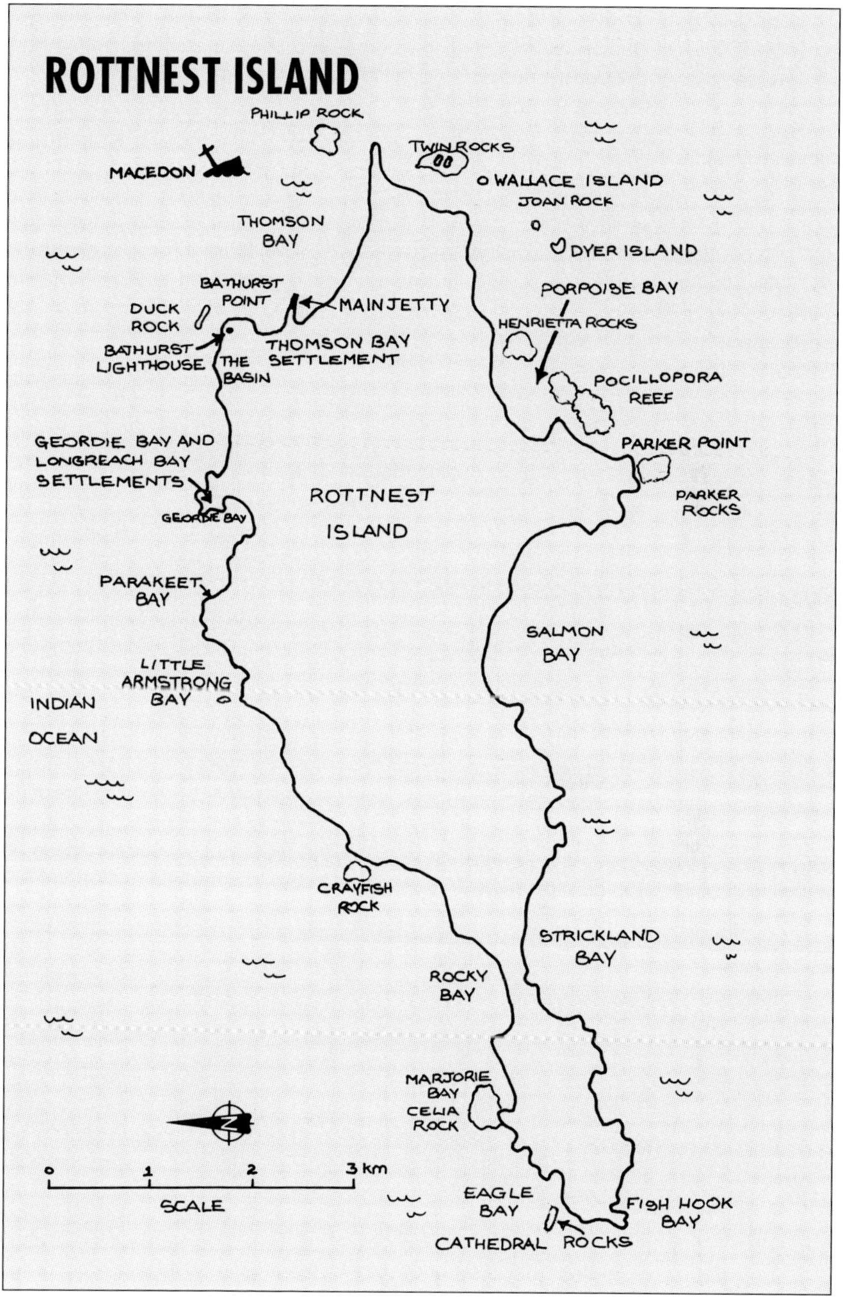
ROTTNEST ISLAND
PHILLIP ROCK
TWIN ROCKS
MACEDON
WALLACE ISLAND
JOAN ROCK
THOMSON BAY
DYER ISLAND
BATHURST POINT
MAIN JETTY
PORPOISE BAY
DUCK ROCK
HENRIETTA ROCKS
BATHURST LIGHTHOUSE
THE BASIN
THOMSON BAY SETTLEMENT
POCILLOPORA REEF
GEORDIE BAY AND LONGREACH BAY SETTLEMENTS
PARKER POINT
GEORDIE BAY
ROTTNEST ISLAND
PARKER ROCKS
PARAKEET BAY
SALMON BAY
LITTLE ARMSTRONG BAY
INDIAN OCEAN
CRAYFISH ROCK
STRICKLAND BAY
ROCKY BAY
MARJORIE BAY
CELIA ROCK
0
1
2
3 km
SCALE
EAGLE BAY
FISH HOOK BAY
CATHEDRAL ROCKS

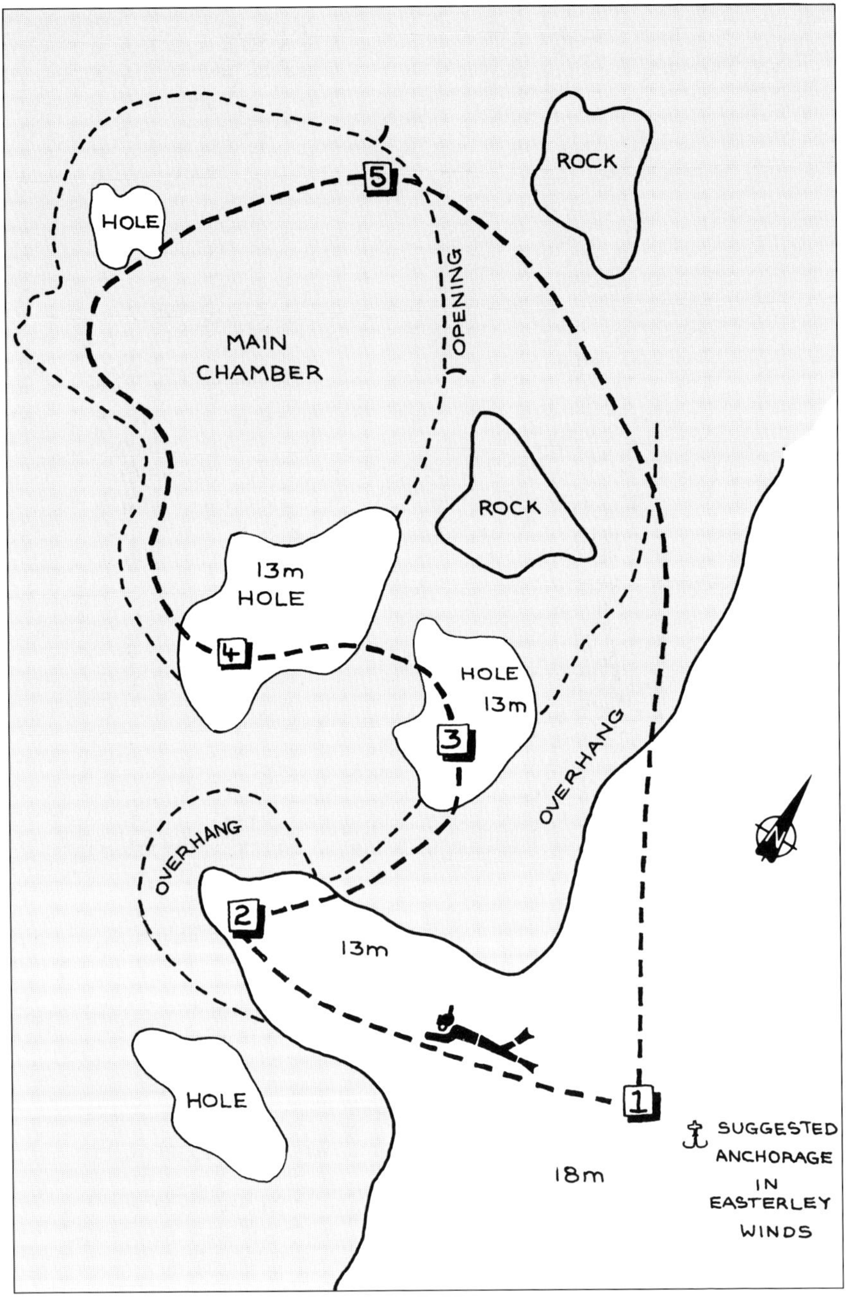
ROCK
HOLE
5
OPENING
MAIN CHAMBER
ROCK
13m HOLE
4
HOLE 13m
3
OVERHANG
OVERHANG
2
13m
HOLE
1
SUGGESTED ANCHORAGE IN EASTERLEY WINDS
18m

Crystal Palace

26

How to get there: *By boat from Rottnest Island or Fremantle.*
Depth: *5-18 metres.*

Crystal Palace consists of three big caves opening out into one another and is remarkable for its sheer scenic grandeur. The site is on the south-east of Rottnest Island, about 1.4 kilometres south of Henrietta Rocks and about 900 metres south-west from Dyer Island. It can be quite difficult to find, as there are no easy reference points nearby and Crystal Palace is not marked on charts. Go to the approximate location, where you are looking for an area about 18 metres deep that rises suddenly to about five metres. If you have GPS on your boat the task will be easier, as it can be found at about latitude 32° 01.601 south and longitude 115° 32.623 east.

1 & 2. In easterly winds, anchor in the sandy area just to the south-east and swim west into a small canyon in the reef, which has an overhang at the rear.
3. Explore a large overhang to the north, which opens into a large hole in the reef. Swim up through the hole and then over the reef (about five metres deep at this point), and drop down into another 13 metre hole.
4. You will find yourself in a huge chamber packed with a diversity of marine life. Two large holes in its roof allow light to stream into the "Palace". Common fish species to be seen include red-lipped morwong, western foxfish, goatfish, common and western scalyfin, common and rough bullseyes, western blue devils, buffalo bream, banded sweep, crested morwong, western talma, horseshoe leatherjackets, white-barred boxfish and black-headed pullers. Other interesting animals sometimes seen here include green turtles, cuttlefish and cowries.
5. Circumnavigate the chamber, exploring interesting nooks and crannies. When you come to a large opening to the north east, swim through it to reach a more northerly section of the large overhang you initially negotiated, and thence return to your boat.

Caution areas: *Beware of boat traffic and do not surface too far from your boat.*
Degree of difficulty: *Moderate.*
Area's status: *The waters around Rottnest are an important marine reserve.*

Adam Meyer, Carolyn Thomson-Dans and Peter Dans

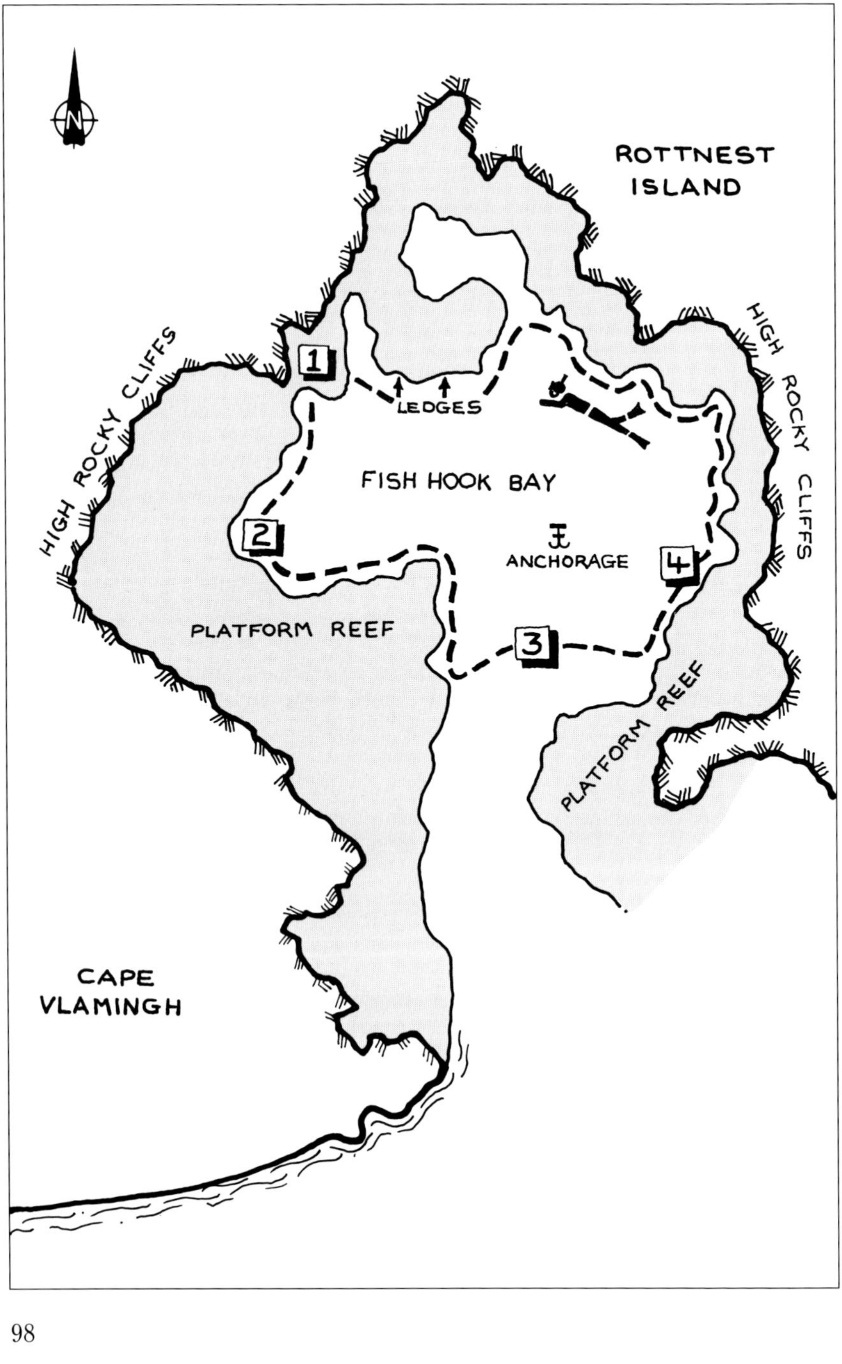
N
ROTTNEST
ISLAND
HIGH ROCKY CLIFFS
HIGH ROCKY CLIFFS
1
LEDGES
FISH HOOK BAY
2
ANCHORAGE
4
PLATFORM REEF
3
PLATFORM REEF
CAPE
VLAMINGH

Fish Hook Bay

27

How to get there: *By boat from Rottnest Island or Fremantle. Access from the island is not permitted.*
Depth: *1-5 metres.*

Fish Hook Bay is one of the most delightful places to snorkel at Rottnest. Surrounded by high limestone cliffs, the bay is visually stunning, has abundant and interesting marine life and water in blue and green hues that is usually crystal clear during summer. It is also rimmed with a reef platform that is riddled with caves, ledges and overhangs. Although it is not deep it would also be worthwhile to explore on SCUBA, because of the caves and other underwater structures.

1. Anchor your boat in the sand in the middle of the bay. However, holding here is poor, so take care to ensure your anchor is set well and always leave someone in the boat. Begin at the reef platform to the north-west. Even the shallow areas around here contain interesting molluscs and other creatures.
2. Just beyond is an area with interesting caves, ledges and overhangs inhabited by colourful moon wrasse, scalyfin and other reef fish. Spend some time exploring this area.
3. As you make your way across the bay you could spot a large dusky morwong lurking on the sand. King George whiting, recognised by the small brown spots on their streamlined silvery bodies, also patrol the sandy areas ready to swoop on tasty morsels.
4. On the eastern side of the bay, the reef walls drop straight down. Make your way around the reef edge to the starting point, stopping to examine other marine life.

Degree of difficulty: *Easy to moderate, depending on conditions.*
Area's status: *The waters around Rottnest are an important marine reserve.*

Carolyn Thomson-Dans and Peter Dans

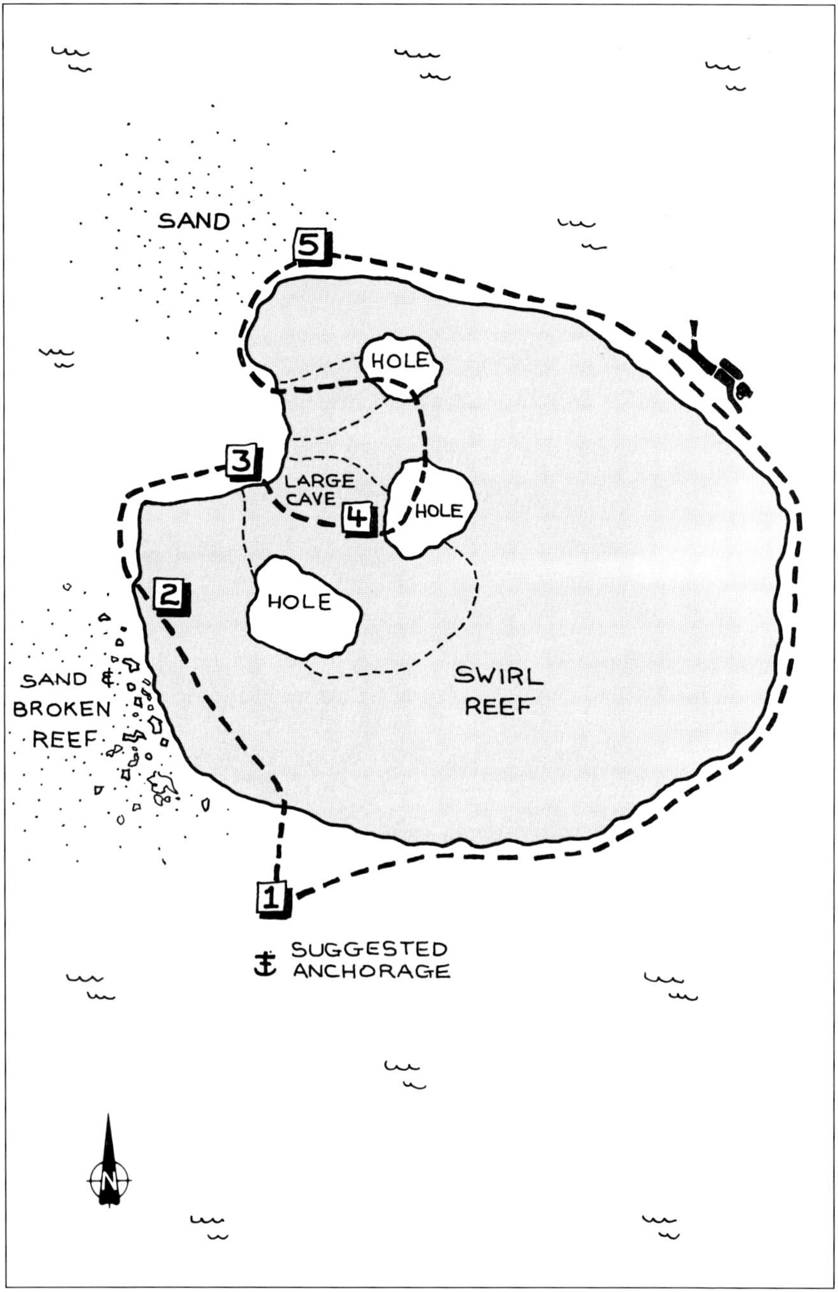
SAND
5
HOLE
3
LARGE CAVE
4
HOLE
2
HOLE
SAND & BROKEN REEF
SWIRL REEF
1
SUGGESTED ANCHORAGE
N

Swirl Reef

How to get there: *By boat from Rottnest Island or Fremantle.*
Depth: *16 metres.*

Like Crystal Palace, Swirl Reef is a magnificent site that is not heavily dived, but it is marked on charts and is considerably easier to find. It is about 1.5 kilometres north of Abraham Point (Marjorie Bay) at about latitude 32° 00' south and longitude 115° 28' east. It is basically a large bombie, with some particularly spectacular caves on its northern side.

1. It is suggested that you anchor in the sand, just to the west of the reef. The western edge of Swirl Reef consists of high broken reef dominated by brown algae communities of kelp and sargassum.
2. Continue in a clockwise direction until you drop off down the side into about 16 metres of water.
3. You will soon encounter the opening of the main gallery at the foot of the reef on the northern side. It is well-lit, with large holes in the roof that allow the light to shoot through. A blue groper often lurks in this spectacular cave. The chance of seeing such a large and magnificent fish in its natural environment is one of the highlights of diving south of the Abrolhos, although adults are now rarely seen on the western coast of Western Australia because of intense fishing. The common blue and orange sea slug (*Chromodoris westraliensis*) is also abundant in this cave, so take a close look at the floor of the cave to see how many you can see.
4. At the back of this large cave you may swim up into another couple of smaller caverns. The fish life in this network of caves is abundant and diverse, and includes schools of bullseyes and old wives. There are numerous wrasse, including scribbled chisel-toothed wrasse, with their blue colouring and Maori-like facial patterns. Other species include horseshoe leatherjackets, blue-lined leatherjackets, western talma, white-banded boxfish, western foxfish, black-headed pullers, banded sweep, herring cale, Woodward's pomfret, zebra fish, moonlighters and red-lipped morwongs. Brightly coloured blue and yellow juvenile scalyfin add a further splash of colour.
5. After leaving the caves to continue around the reef in a clockwise direction, keep your eyes open for stingrays that inhabit the sand around the perimeter. Most

have venomous spines attached to the tail, but they are not usually aggressive. The rest of the dive is predominantly high broken reef of differing levels, with large potholes that are worthy of further investigation.

Degree of difficulty: *Moderate to difficult, depending on conditions.*
Area's status: *The waters around Rottnest are an important marine reserve.*

Peter Dans, Carolyn Thomson-Dans and Adam Meyer

SUNFISH

From time to time, a huge dorsal fin is spotted just offshore from swimming beaches in Perth's metropolitan area, triggering great alarm. Sometimes the innocent cause of this panic is one of our most fascinating, rarely seen and completely harmless animals - the sunfish.

Sunfish are oceanic creatures but they enter coastal waters on rare occasions, perhaps in search of the jellyfish that form their staple diet. They also consume salps, comb jellies, young fish and small crustaceans. Some species can weigh more than two tonnes and attain lengths of three metres, but all sunfish have a very stumpy rear end, with an extremely short tail fin. To compensate, the large dorsal and anal fins are both positioned at the end of the body.

Two species of sunfish enter the waters near Perth. The short sunfish is found around the entire coast of Australia, and the even more curious oblong sunfish is found around the State's southern half. Schools of this species have even thrown themselves ashore in the Albany area. Their nearest relatives are porcupinefish and pufferfish.

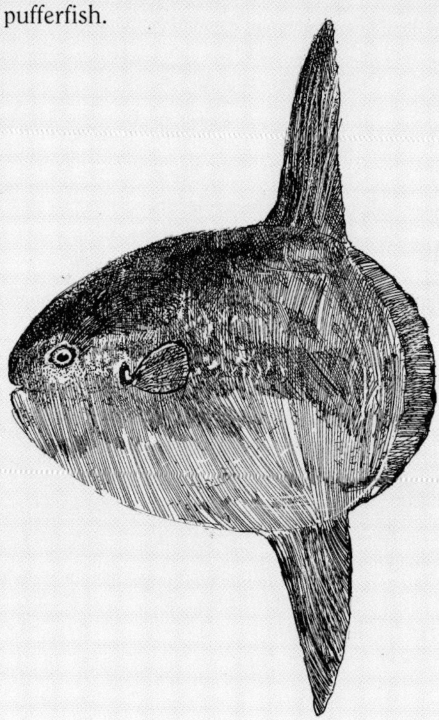

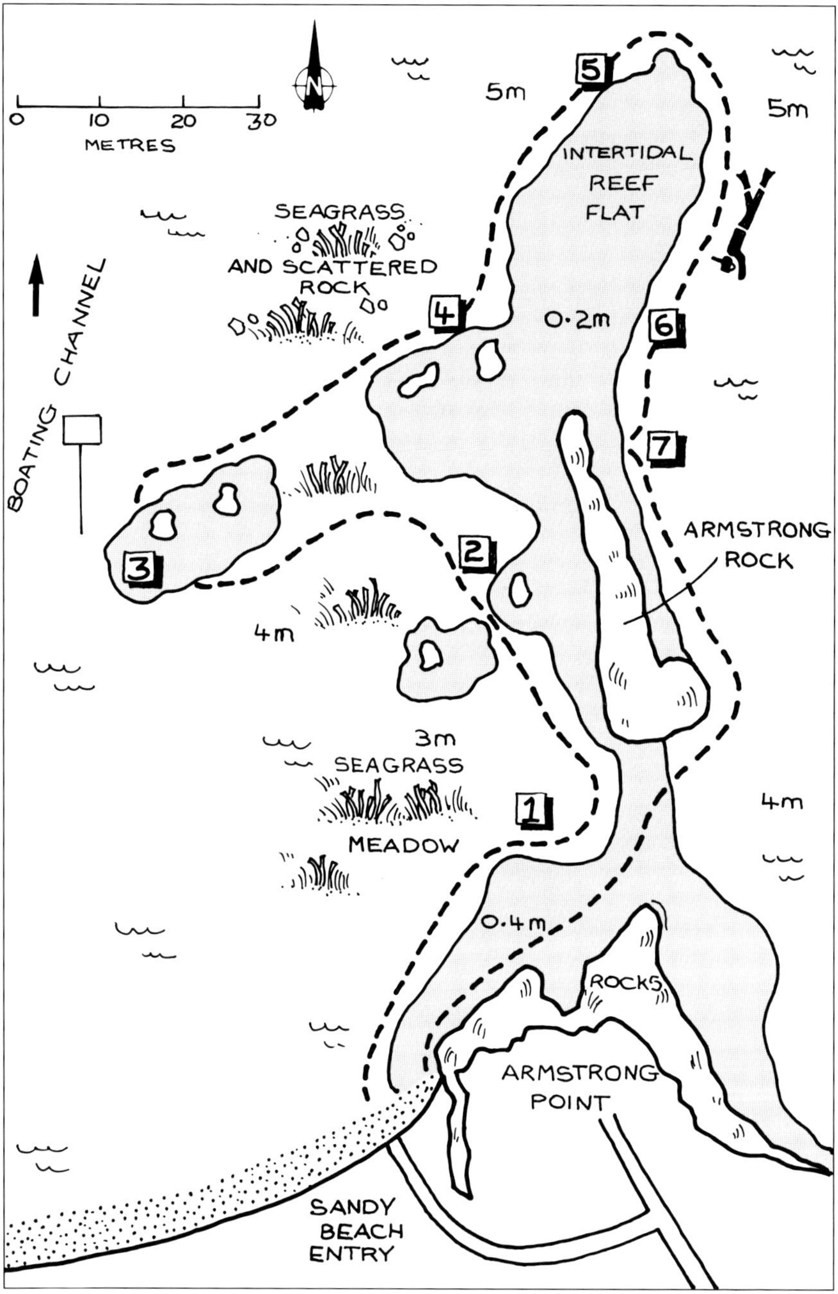

0
10
20
30
METRES
N
5m
5m
5
INTERTIDAL
REEF
FLAT
SEAGRASS
AND SCATTERED
ROCK
BOATING CHANNEL
4
0·2m
6
7
ARMSTRONG
ROCK
3
2
4m
3m
SEAGRASS
MEADOW
1
4m
0·4m
ROCKS
ARMSTRONG
POINT
SANDY
BEACH
ENTRY

Armstrong Point

29

How to get there: *By bus from Thomson Bay.*
Depth: *3-5 metres.*

Armstrong Point is an ideal area for snorkellers, with some good underwater scenery, and would be excellent for beginners (other than children). If you become tired, you are able to get out anywhere you like and rest on the reef platform.

1. Entry is from a sandy beach just west of Armstrong Point. Follow the reef platform. As you head out, there is a meadow of wireweed (*Amphibolis*) seagrass to your left. In this area you may see some black and white striped zebra fish.
2. A gap in the reef platform adjacent to Armstrong Rock provides some nice holes and swimthroughs.
3. Next, head to a nice bombie to the north-west, but take care as it is close to a boating channel. Fish species you may see on this dive include black-spotted goatfish, Brownfield's wrasse and western king wrasse.
4. Back on the main reef platform, there are some reasonably large caves, inhabited by western buffalo bream and other fish species.
5. At the most seaward point of the reef there are some interesting walls with colourful sponge growth. This is a good place to try and spot delicate blue and orange nudibranchs (*Chromodoris westraliensis*).
6. Heading back along the other side of the reef flat, there are more caves and undercut ledges.
7. The reef platform on the eastern side of Armstrong Rock would make an ideal place to rest for awhile, before you complete the dive. After a short break, continue south alongside Armstrong Rock, then make your way back to the entry point by swimming over the reef flat and hence back to the sandy beach.

Caution areas: *Beware of boat traffic and always tow a dive flag to warn boaters of your presence.*
Degree of difficulty: *Easy to moderate, depending on conditions.*
Area's status: *The waters around Rottnest are an important marine reserve.*

Mike Lapwood, Carolyn Williams and Tim Daly

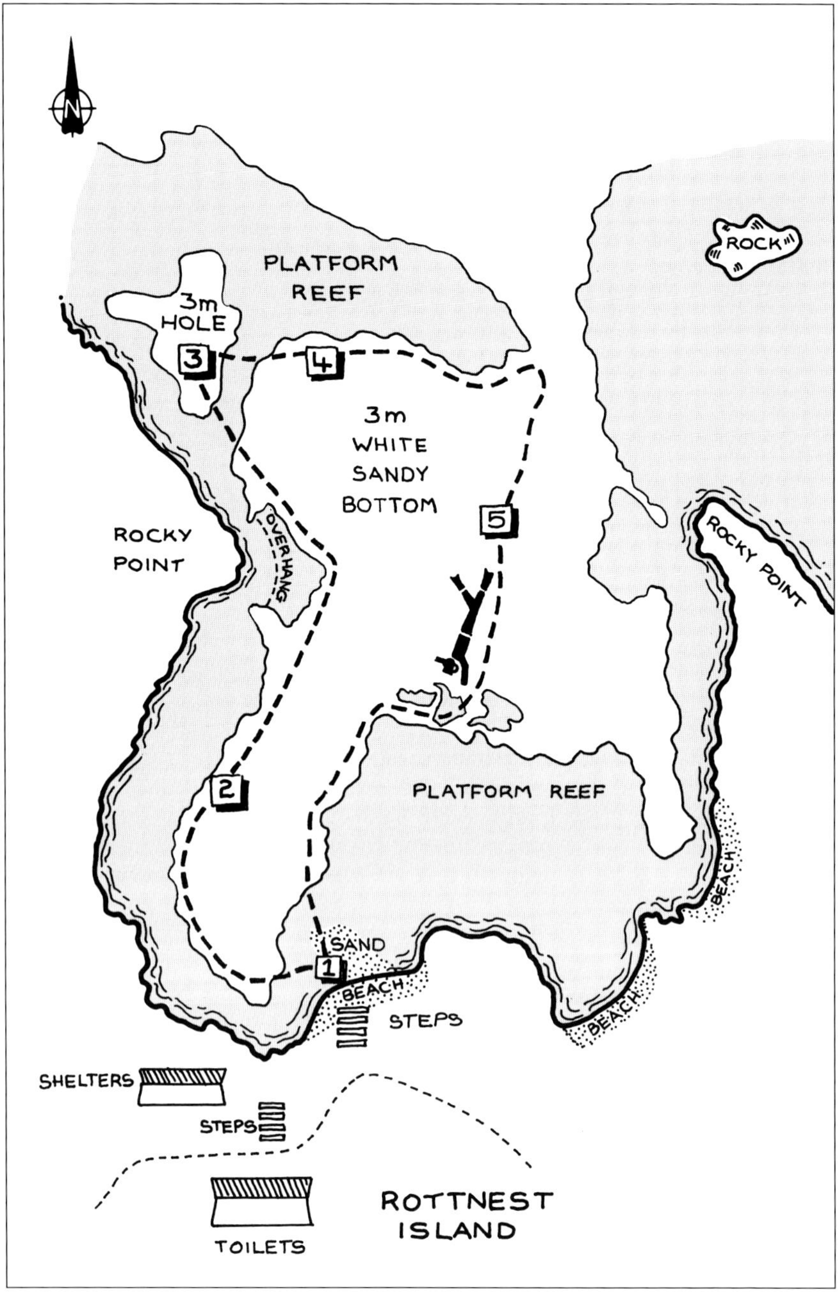
N
PLATFORM REEF
3m HOLE
ROCK
3
4
3m WHITE SANDY BOTTOM
5
ROCKY POINT
OVERHANG
ROCKY POINT
2
PLATFORM REEF
SAND
1
BEACH
BEACH
BEACH
STEPS
SHELTERS
STEPS
TOILETS
ROTTNEST ISLAND

The Basin

30

How to get there: *The Basin is an easy bike ride or 10 minute walk from the settlement at Thomson Bay.*
Depth: *1-3 metres.*

Easily the most popular swimming and snorkelling area on Rottnest Island, the Basin is on the north-eastern side of the island, 500 metres west of the Bathurst lighthouse. Facilities include a freshwater shower, tables, a drinking fountain, toilets (suitable for people with disabilities) and bike racks. The site is ideal for novice snorkellers and is suitable for the whole family. As a snorkelling site it is unbeatable for ease of access and for the abundance and variety of species. The Basin is protected from the south-westerly sea breeze, but is open to north-westerly winds and swell.

1. Begin at the beach, near the steps. Aptly named, this site is a basin between well-developed platform reefs on either side of the bay.
2. As you swim along the shallow reef edge, watch out for small fish such as hardyheads and stripeys. As the water becomes a little deeper, you may see a juvenile western rock lobster.
3. Look for the deep hole on the left hand edge of the reef platform. Buffalo bream and red-lipped morwong feed along the three metre high reef wall faces. Small corals and coralline algae can be seen on the reef walls. Spend some time at this hole, as what you will find may surprise you. Fish include banded sweep, scalyfins, cardinalfish, various wrasse species, sea carp, western blue devils, herring and old wives. Look for the trails of molluscs in the sand.
4. As you come out of the hole, continue to follow the reef edge. Watch the top of the platform, as the broken reef has many interesting signs of marine life.
5. To return, swim across the sand towards the beach, looking for small flatheads and black-spotted goatfish. Along the reef edge, you will find small channels and gullies that bisect the reef platform. Swim over these channels, looking for the secretive small fish and colourful nudibranchs (sea slugs) that enjoy their protection.

Degree of difficulty: *Easy.*
Area's status: *The waters around Rottnest are an important marine reserve. No fishing is allowed in the Basin during daylight hours.*

Peter Lambert, John Edwards and Paul Finlay

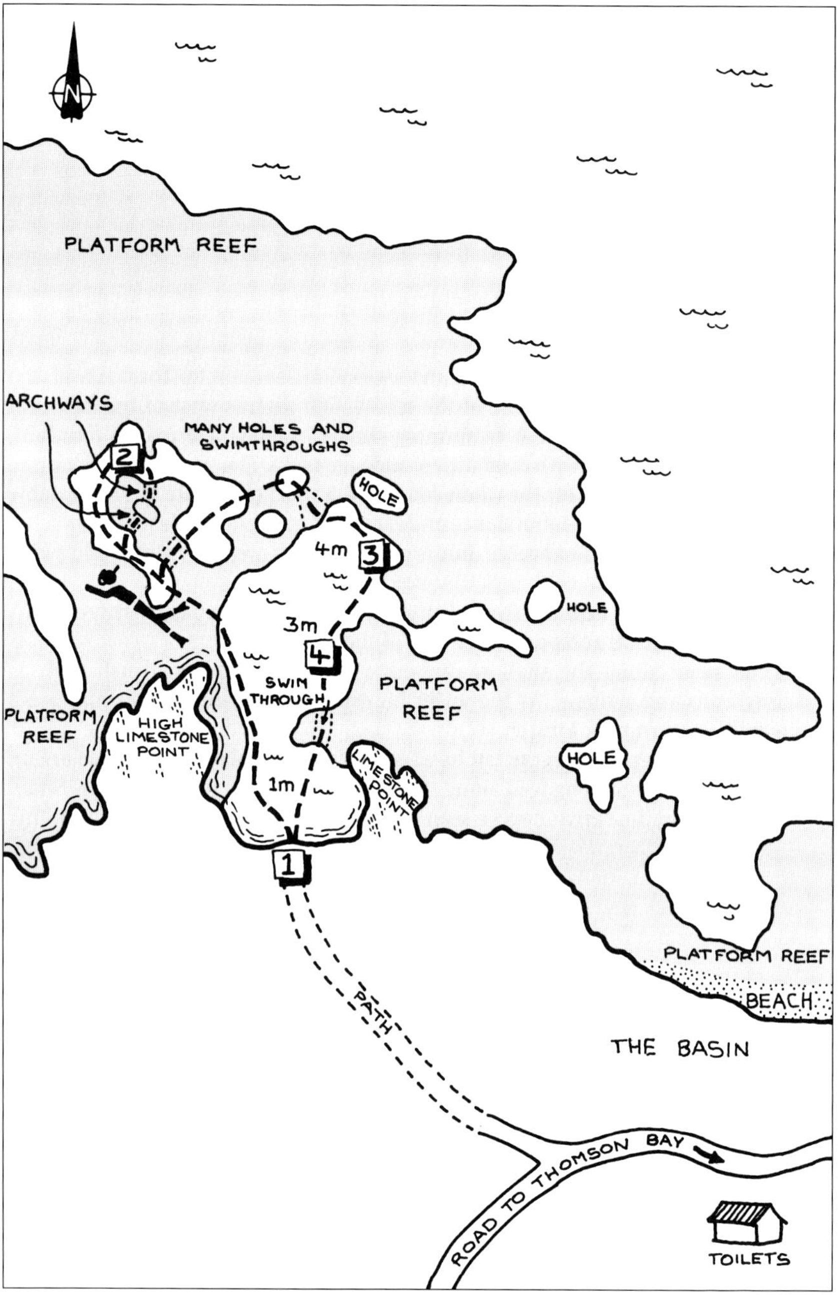
N
PLATFORM REEF
ARCHWAYS
MANY HOLES AND SWIMTHROUGHS
HOLE
2
3
4m
3m
4
HOLE
SWIM THROUGH
PLATFORM REEF
PLATFORM REEF
HIGH LIMESTONE POINT
1m
LIMESTONE POINT
HOLE
1
PLATFORM REEF
BEACH
PATH
THE BASIN
ROAD TO THOMSON BAY
TOILETS

West of the Basin

31

How to get there: *The Basin is an easy bike ride or 10 minute walk from the settlement at Thomson Bay.*
Depth: *1-4 metres.*

After the kids have enjoyed a swim at the Basin, mum and dad may choose a more advanced snorkelling adventure to be found just around the corner. Apart from the many and varied fish species that can be found here, the advanced snorkeller will enjoy the many swimthroughs that link the pools off the headland that separates the Basin and Longreach Bay. However, don't attempt this site unless you are an advanced snorkeller and there are calm to mild weather conditions, with little or no swell. To reach the site, take the path that heads up the limestone headland west of the Basin.

1. The best entry point to the main pool is from the rocky shoreline at the end of the track. Make your way around the reef along the western side of the pool, where you will cross an interesting combination of seagrasses, rock, sponges and sand. See if you can see limpets in the rocky intertidal zone, and possibly sea slugs.
2. Explore an area where the shallow reef is riddled with gullies, spectacular holes, swimthroughs and arches. Black-spotted goatfish, buffalo bream, whiting, red-striped cardinalfish, bullseyes, prettyfins, truncate coralfish, sea carp, zebra fish and slender wrasse abound amongst a diversity of other marine life, including some splendid examples of kelp and sargassum.
3. Return to the northern end of the main pool, where there are further holes and ledges to investigate. In a few places you can see small clumps of pink pocillopora coral (*Pocillopora damicornis*). Rottnest Island is the southernmost location that this species is known to grow.
4. Negotiate a final swimthrough before returning to your starting point. Alternatively, you could swim around the limestone point and return to the main Basin beach along the edge of the platform reef.

Degree of difficulty: *On a good day this is easy to moderately difficult. However, in rough conditions and swell it would be difficult.*
Area's status: *The waters around Rottnest are an important marine reserve. No fishing is allowed in the Basin during daylight hours.*

Peter Lambert, John Edwards and Paul Finlay

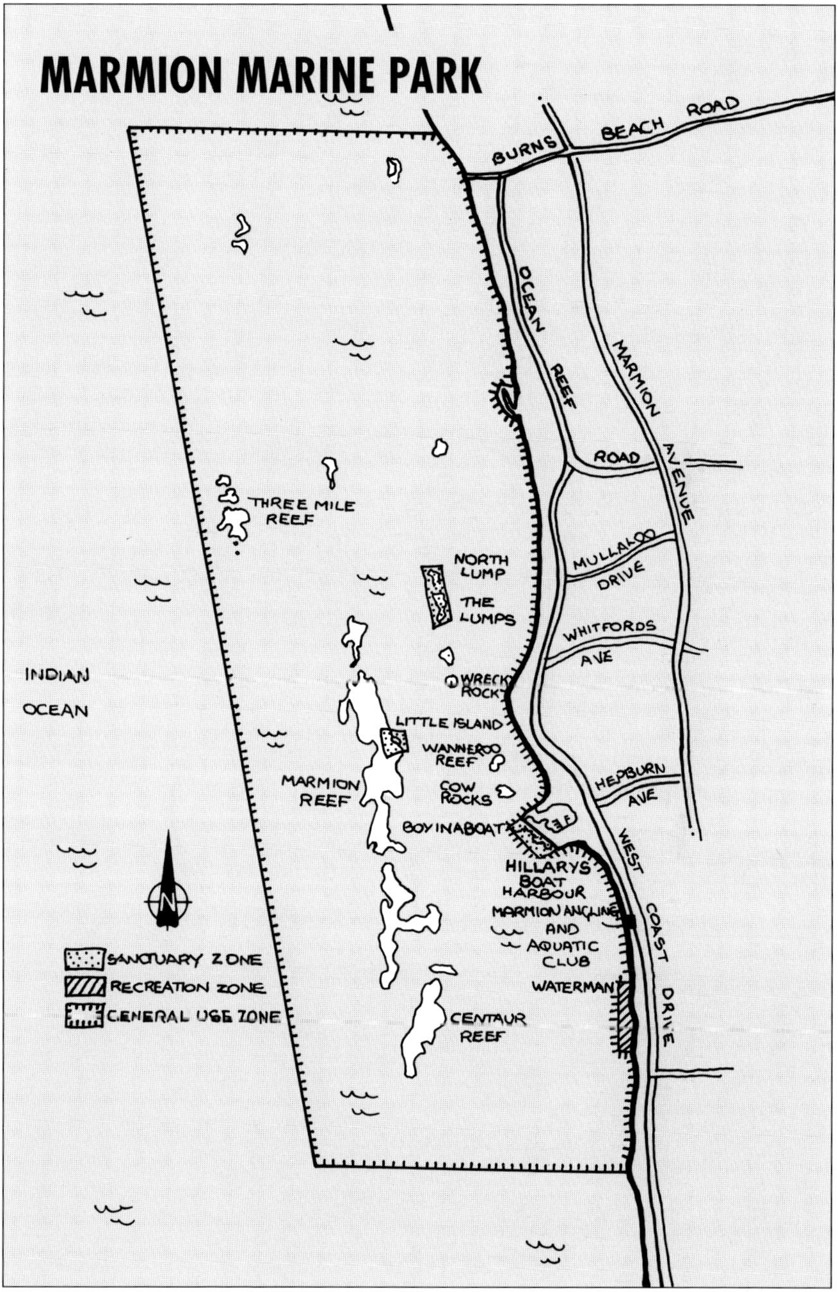
MARMION MARINE PARK
BURNS BEACH ROAD
OCEAN REEF ROAD
MARMION AVENUE
THREE MILE REEF
NORTH LUMP
THE LUMPS
MULLALOO DRIVE
WHITFORDS AVE
INDIAN OCEAN
WRECK ROCK
LITTLE ISLAND
WANNEROO REEF
MARMION REEF
COW ROCKS
BOYINABOAT
HEPBURN AVE
HILLARYS BOAT HARBOUR
MARMION ANGLING AND AQUATIC CLUB
WEST COAST DRIVE
WATERMAN
CENTAUR REEF
SANCTUARY ZONE
RECREATION ZONE
GENERAL USE ZONE

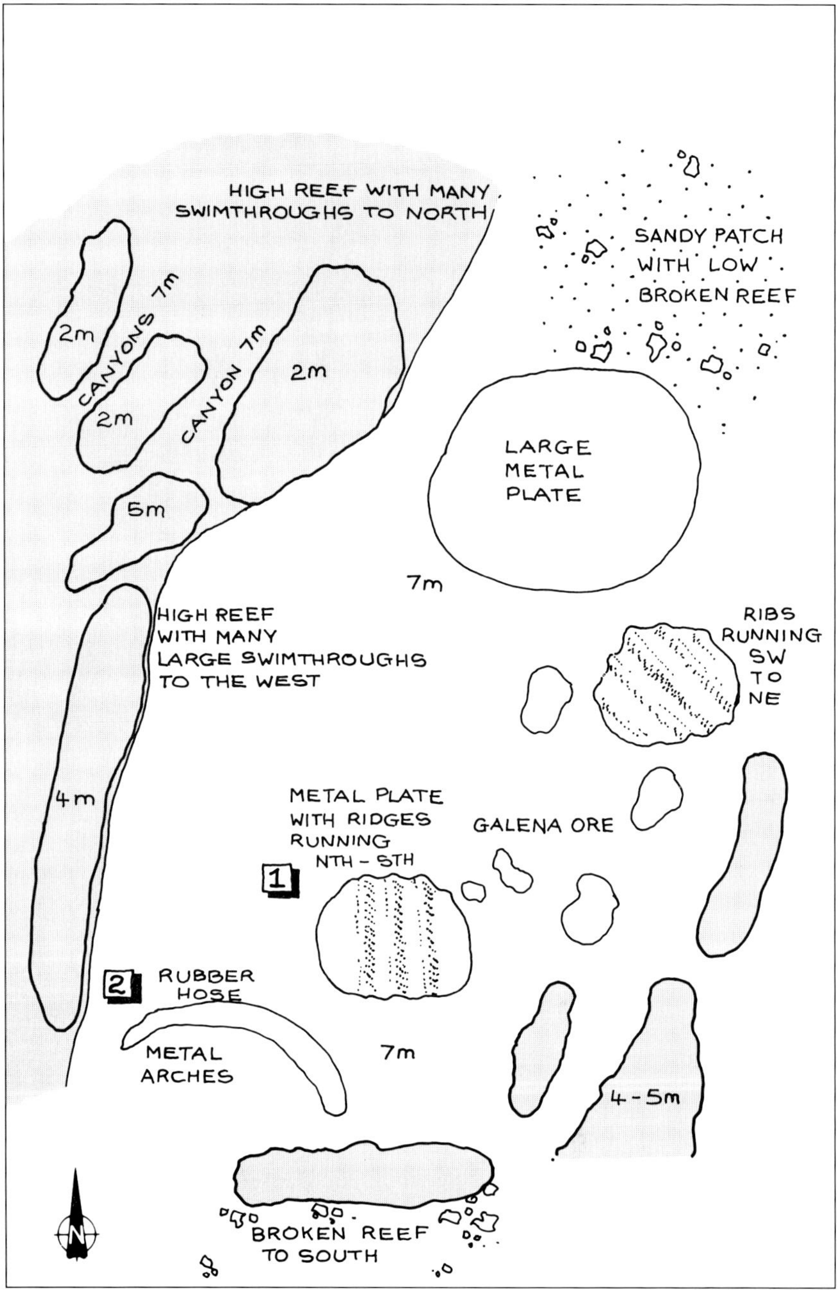
HIGH REEF WITH MANY SWIMTHROUGHS TO NORTH
SANDY PATCH WITH LOW BROKEN REEF
2m
CANYONS 7m
CANYON 7m
2m
2m
5m
LARGE METAL PLATE
7m
HIGH REEF WITH MANY LARGE SWIMTHROUGHS TO THE WEST
RIBS RUNNING SW TO NE
4m
METAL PLATE WITH RIDGES RUNNING NTH - STH
GALENA ORE
1
2
RUBBER HOSE
METAL ARCHES
7m
4-5m
BROKEN REEF TO SOUTH
N

Centaur Wreck

32

How to get there: *By boat from Hillarys Boat Harbour.*
Depth: *Maximum of 9 metres.*
Coordinates: *Latitude 31° 51.83 south, longitude 115° 42.67 east.*
Chart: *Centaur Reef is marked on DMH 150.*

This dive offers the best of both worlds - historic and interesting wreck remains lie scattered around Centaur Reef, which is riddled with spectacular swimthroughs and gullies. The *Centaur* struck the southernmost section of the reef on December 9, 1874, while en route to Fremantle. It is immediately west of Hamersley Street in North Beach, about 3.7 kilometres offshore.

1. The wreck itself is encrusted with marine organisms, making it somewhat difficult to distinguish from the surrounding reef. When searching for it, look for objects which look unnatural or man-made. A large encrusted metal plate with three distinct ridges is relatively easy to locate. The 30-metre-long iron brig played an important role in the development of the infant colony of Western Australia, transporting galena (lead ore) from Champion Bay (Geraldton), which was then a thriving mining area, via Fremantle to Melbourne. It brought back vital supplies such as spirits, tobacco, nails, wagons, angora goats, and the colony's first quartz crushing battery in readiness for the anticipated gold boom.
2. Close by is a rubber hose and small amounts of galena ore, which have weathered to a grey to light purple. The *Centaur* was carrying 200 tonnes of galena when it struck the reef at six and a half knots and became impaled on it, but much of this was subsequently salvaged. The nine crew and four passengers on board were able to scramble to safety, but five minutes after the lifeboats pulled away the ship crashed over and largely disappeared from view. At a subsequent inquiry the Captain, Frederick Brabham, was criticised for bringing the vessel too near the coast, and his license was suspended for three months.
3. Swim to the west of the wreck to locate a high reef that contains many large swimthroughs. There are numerous large wrasse and a diversity of wrasse species, including maori, senator, brown-spotted, western king and Brownfield's. Take some time to note the many different forms. Other fish life includes western talma, western sea carp, moonlighters, western blue devils, banded toadfish, dusky morwongs, banded sweep, western scalyfins, McCulloch's scalyfins and red-lipped morwongs. Schools of yellowtail scad, buffalo bream, silver drummers and bullseyes also inhabit the area.

4. There is a high reef to the north, with many swimthroughs and deeply eroded canyons and gullies. This is a very rewarding area to explore but is also subject to the most surge, so take care. There are many delicate gorgonian fan corals, strategically positioned to take advantage of currents that carry food to their mouths. Colonies of transparent sea squirts are also present in high numbers. Sponges of many forms and colours encrust the reef, including many with beautiful pastel shades. Under some ledges numerous large dead shells, including turban shells and whelks, have been collected over time. Other invertebrates include some very large sea urchins wedged into crevices, sea tulips and at least two different species of nudibranchs.

Caution areas: *Centaur Reef can experience strong surge, especially if there is any sort of swell, so it is recommended that you dive it only in optimum conditions.*
Degree of difficulty: *Moderate to difficult, depending on conditions.*
Area's status: *Lies within the Marmion Marine Park. The* Centaur *is also a protected wreck site and artefacts can't be removed from the area.*

Kevin Crane, Carolyn Thomson-Dans, Brad Daw and Peter Dans

SEAGRASSES

All animal life in the ocean is in some way linked to marine plants. Seagrasses, in particular, provide an important food source and shelter for marine organisms. These carpets of life grow in sheltered and shallow waters throughout the world, except for Antarctica. About 50 species of seagrass grow worldwide. Australia has 31 species, more than any other continent, and 14 of these grow in the Perth region. New Zealand, in stark contrast to Australia, has only two species of seagrass growing in its waters.

Unlike seaweeds, with which they are often confused, seagrasses are true flowering plants that have a root system that grows on and stabilises sand. Seagrass meadows provide an important food source and habitat for hundreds of animals and help to stabilise the sea floor. Such beds attract a wide range of animals, such as tiny worms, molluscs, echinoderms and crustaceans. These in turn attract larger animals and so begins a complex food web. The importance of this cannot be underestimated. Seagrass beds provide nursery areas for many commercially important species, including western rock lobsters and tiger prawns.

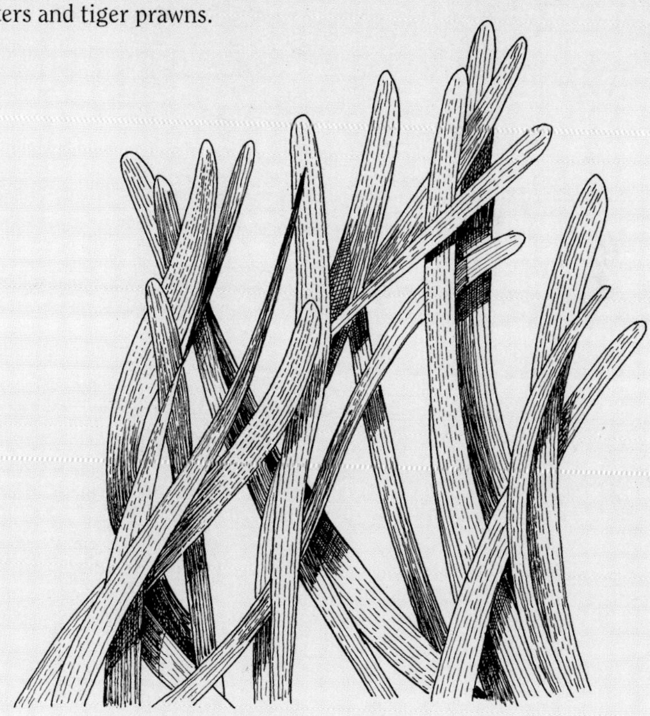

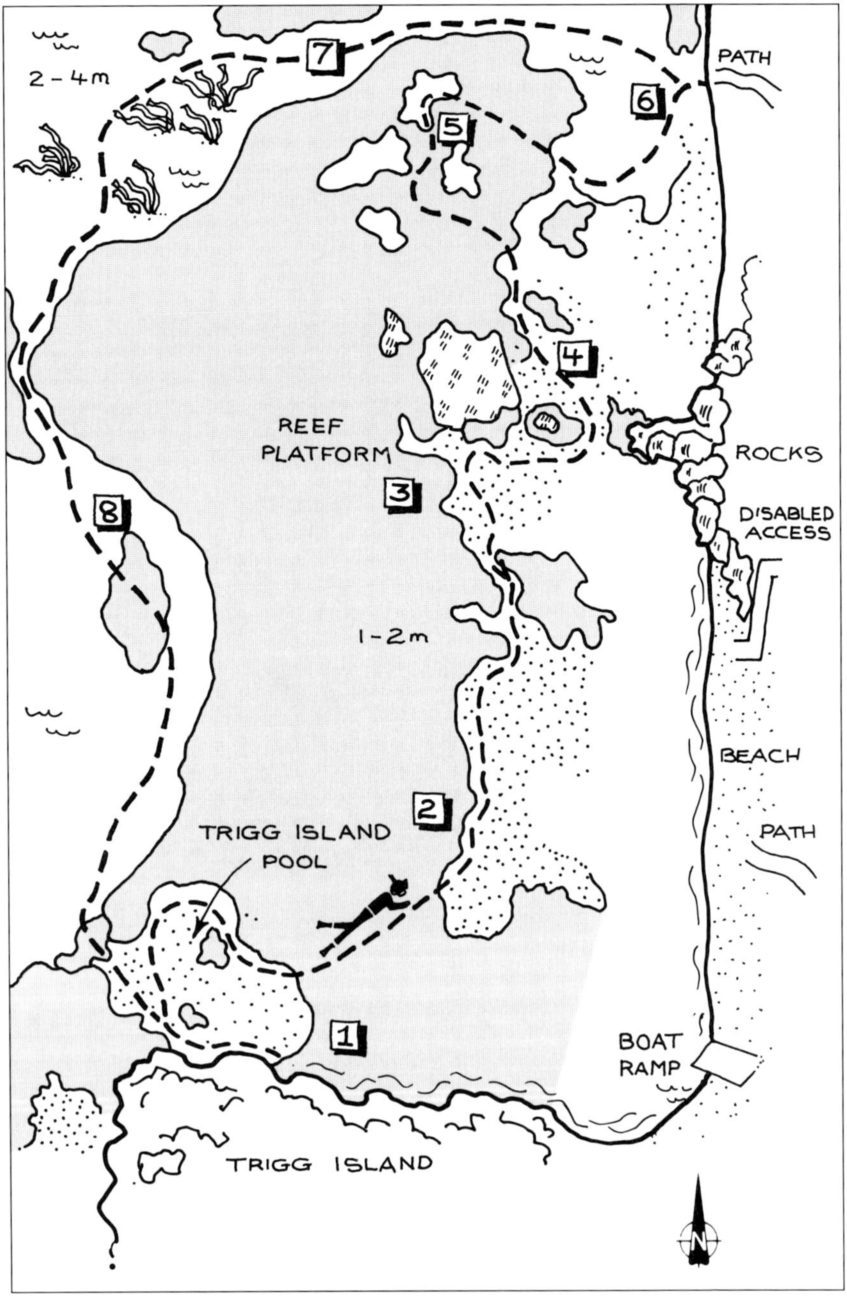
2 – 4m
7
PATH
6
5
4
REEF
PLATFORM
ROCKS
3
8
DISABLED
ACCESS
1 – 2m
BEACH
2
PATH
TRIGG ISLAND
POOL
1
BOAT
RAMP
TRIGG ISLAND
N

Trigg Island

33

How to get there: *Turn west into the Esplanade off West Coast Drive and park in the northern car park between Clarko Reserve and the beach.*
Depth: *1-4 metres.*

The reef platform north of Trigg Island provides a safe and interesting environment to learn to snorkel, and has access for divers or snorkellers with disabilities. This site can be subject to large swells, so if you intend to snorkel beyond the reef platform choose a day with fine conditions and a low swell.

1. A light current flows through the small lagoon from south to north, so enter the water near the island and drift slowly north after exploring the pool.
2. Swim over a small, shallow reef platform, to find a ledge running north to south. The crevices and overhangs have an array of molluscs, sea stars and urchins.
3. This area is shallow (less than a metre), but dominated by deep crevices and overhangs. Fish include silver drummers, stripeys and red-lipped morwongs.
4. Look through the cave beneath this rock. A school of silver drummers often shelters in this cavern. Sea lettuce covers the reef and common sea hares (*Aplysia dactylomelia*) are often found here in summer.
5. A number of deep pools have formed in the reef platform. Octopus lairs can be found by the tell-tale pile of discarded shells at their entrance. You may also see elephant snails. Their black mantle may be all that is visible in the deep crevices.
6. At this point, novice snorkellers may leave the water and return to the start point or beach. Experienced snorkellers can continue into deeper water.
7. This area has low reef dominated by brown algae, particularly kelp. There are large, undercut ledges on both sides, with numerous sponges and ascidians on their walls. Abalone, chitons and limpets are abundant on the reef top.
8. This area can be badly affected by even a small swell, so don't get too near the edge of the reef platform. Large schools of fish are often seen in this deep pool. You may safely exit the water by returning to Trigg Island Pool and then the beach.

Caution areas: *Don't dive beyond your level of comfort. Be wary of prevailing conditions. Boats may use the ramp near the island, so always tow a flag.*
Degree of difficulty: *Easy to moderate, depending on conditions.*
Area's status: *The area lies within the Marmion Marine Park.*

George Watson

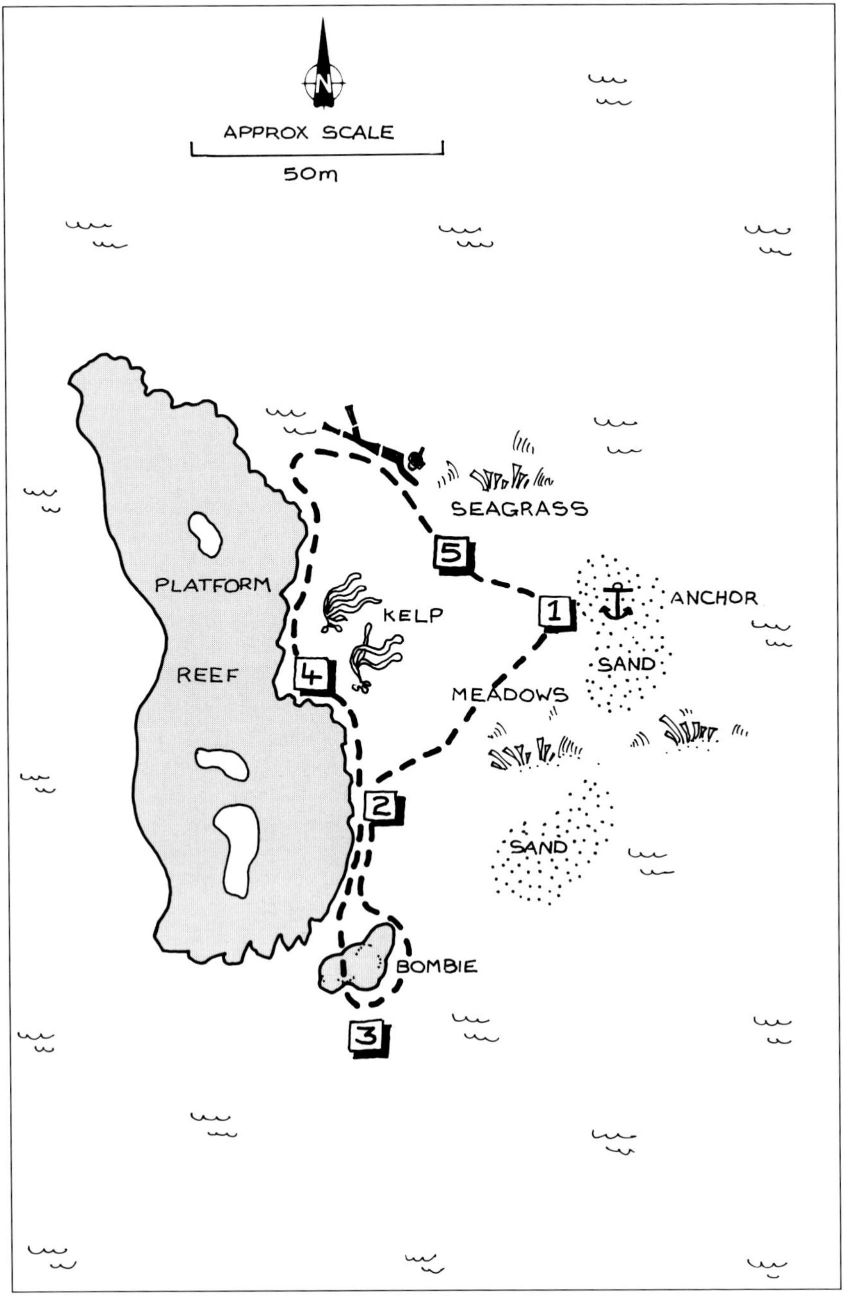
N
APPROX SCALE
50m
SEAGRASS
5
PLATFORM
KELP
1
ANCHOR
REEF
4
SAND
MEADOWS
2
SAND
BOMBIE
3

Burns Rocks

34

How to get there: *By boat from Ocean Reef Harbour, Mullaloo Point or Hillarys Boat Harbour.*
Depth: *3-6 metres.*

Burns Rocks lie at the northern end of the Marmion Marine Park, a little more than one kilometre offshore from the Burns coastal settlement. They cover an area about 150 metres in length and comprise three jagged remnant limestone islets, rising about 2.5 metres above sea level. The islets are set on a reef platform, which is exposed at low tide and skirts the rocks. Access from the south by boat is through the sheltered inshore waters of the marine park. On the inland side of the rocks, vessels are best anchored in one of two sand patches, sheltered from the ocean swells and prevailing sea breezes.

1. Beginning your dive from a sand patch anchorage site, your depth gauge should register about five metres on reaching the bottom. Swimming in a south-westerly direction, you will cross a seagrass meadow of ribbon weed and paddle weed. Seagrass meadows support a wealth of marine creatures and are vitally important to the marine ecosystem. Taking the time to look more closely at these areas, many juvenile species of fish emerge, such as sand whiting and Brownfield's wrasse, along with invertebrates such as molluscs, sea anemones, brittle stars, sea slugs, baler shells and coneshells.
2. Once at the reef platform face, swim to the southern end. Here, the gentle swells wash over the platform reef, and Roe's abalone, sea urchins and sea stars can be seen under the ledges. The overhang of the platform provides an array of small caves and ledges, where fish such as rough bullseyes, scalyfin and cardinalfish peer curiously at the diver.

View of Burns Rocks - east to west

3. An interesting bombie can be explored just off the inside of the southern end of the platform. Circumnavigate the bombie to appreciate the diversity of sea life here, such as crested morwongs, stripeys, colourful orange sponges, tube worms and brown-spotted wrasse.
4. Return to the reef platform face, and follow along the inside to the northern end of the system. Depths are generally shallow along the face, varying from 2 to 4 metres. Here, the reef platform breaks into a series of ledges, overhangs, swimthroughs, gullies, small caves and multi-coloured walls encrusted with sponges, gorgonian sea fans and sea tulips. Remains of lobster pots amongst the kelp signal the presence of lobsters, while rock crabs scurry about close to the platform surface. Closer investigation of these areas reveals curious gobies, which peer from the protection of their rented apartments. At cave entrances and beyond, banded sweep, buffalo bream, fusilier sweep, western blue devils, truncate coralfish and old wives dart about, defending their territories.
5. As you complete the circuit back to the boat, an interesting variety of seagrass meadows and sandy stony bottom will provide a diversity of life, such as zebra fish, western king wrasse, sea pike, skipjack trevally, gobbleguts, and clams.

Caution areas: *Caution should be exercised if you are travelling from Hillarys Boat Harbour or Mullaloo Point, as there are a number of smaller areas of rock and platform reef awash at high tide in these coastal areas.*
Degree of difficulty: *Easy to moderate, depending on conditions.*
Area's status: *Lies within the Marmion Marine Park.*

Peter Lambert, Doug Coughran, John Edwards and Peter Pennings

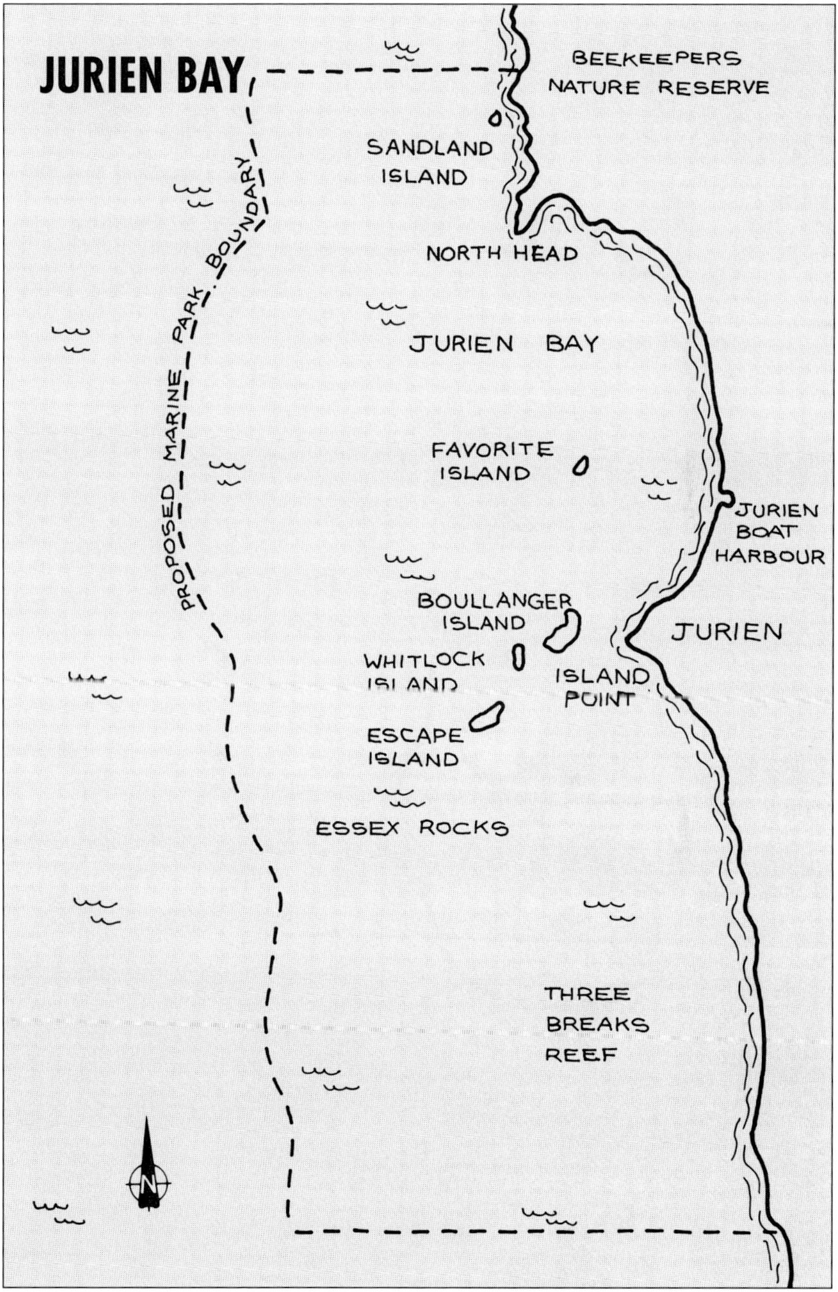
JURIEN BAY
BEEKEEPERS NATURE RESERVE
SANDLAND ISLAND
PROPOSED MARINE PARK BOUNDARY
NORTH HEAD
JURIEN BAY
FAVORITE ISLAND
JURIEN BOAT HARBOUR
BOULLANGER ISLAND
JURIEN
WHITLOCK ISLAND
ISLAND POINT
ESCAPE ISLAND
ESSEX ROCKS
THREE BREAKS REEF
N

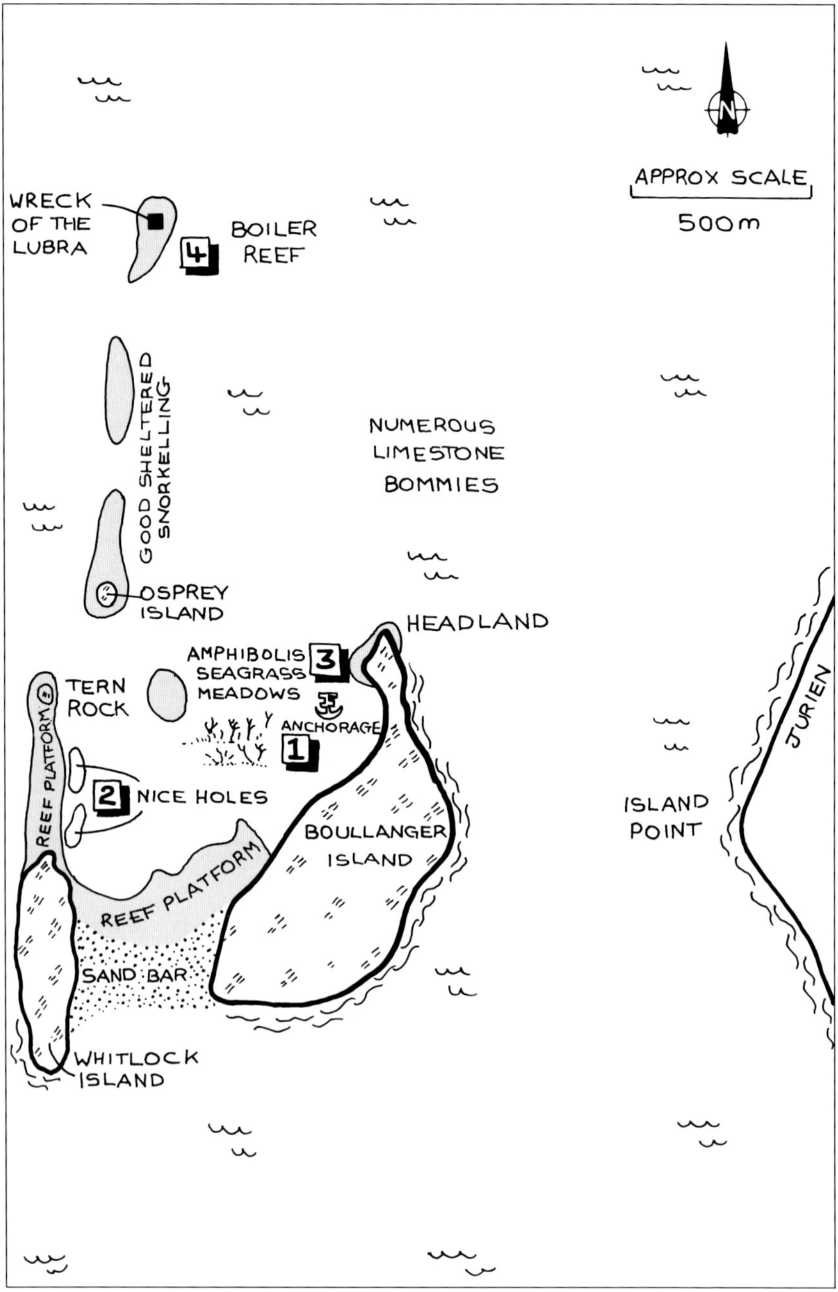
APPROX SCALE
500m
N
WRECK OF THE LUBRA
4
BOILER REEF
GOOD SHELTERED SNORKELLING
NUMEROUS LIMESTONE BOMMIES
OSPREY ISLAND
HEADLAND
AMPHIBOLIS SEAGRASS MEADOWS
3
TERN ROCK
ANCHORAGE
1
REEF PLATFORM
2
NICE HOLES
JURIEN
ISLAND POINT
BOULLANGER ISLAND
REEF PLATFORM
SAND BAR
WHITLOCK ISLAND

Boullanger Island

How to get there: *Access is via boat from the Jurien Marina or small boats can be launched at the point from Shingle Ave.*
Depth: *1-6 metres.*
Chart: *DMH 171.*

Boullanger Island is one kilometre offshore from Island Point, at the southern end of Jurien Bay. It is the closest of three islands that afford some great diving and sheltered anchorages. The back of Boullanger Island is a great spot for family groups to go snorkelling.

AREA 1

The lagoon behind Boullanger Island provides a shallow, protected anchorage with extensive seagrass meadows of wireweed (*Amphibolis*) and limestone bombies in three to four metres of water. The entire area is bordered by the island on the eastern and southern sides and a limestone intertidal reef platform on the western side blocks any swell. A craggy rock outcrop (Osprey Island) stands sentinel-like along the reef, and a smaller rock is visible further south (Tern Island).

1. Anchor in the lagoon near the headland of Boullanger Island.
2. Swim to the south-western corner of the lagoon, where there is a series of holes and overhangs that open up into huge caves. It is almost impossible to get a boat in here because it is so shallow, but at low tide you can walk to this area across the reef. There is plenty of pocillopora coral, a hard pink coral that is very attractive. It is possible in some places to swim through the caves to the outside of the reef, but this depends very much on the swell. However, a SCUBA dive on the reef is well worth the effort.
3. Before you return to your boat, the northern headland of Boullanger Island is also worth a swim and Australian sea lions will often join you. However, because they can sometimes be dangerous, do not approach them and never attempt to touch a sea lion. Keep your hands close to your body and your movements to a minimum, to avoid startling the animal. If a sea lion becomes overly aggressive (such as nipping at your flippers or nudging your body) you should move away cautiously and leave the water.

The entire area between the headland, Osprey Island and Boullanger Island is a settlement area for western rock lobster puerulus (the next stage after the larval stage), and the settlement mats are marked by floats. Please do not disturb the mats in any way, as valuable fisheries data is collected from them.

AREA 2

4. If you follow the inside of the reef platform for about two kilometres north from the western edge of the lagoon, you will see the "boiler" on Boiler Reef. Divers need to be strong swimmers to attempt this, as it is quite a lengthy swim, and most people would find it preferable to take their boat. This boiler is, in fact, the massive engine block of the ill-fated passenger steamship *Lubra*, wrecked in 1898. The remains of the steel vessel are scattered over a wide area and make an interesting dive, with plenty of "crays" in and under the steel plates. The remains are gazetted under the Historic Shipwrecks Act so please look, but don't take.

Caution areas: *Avoid the seaward side of the reef if any swell is running. Swimming into caves and under ledges can be hazardous.*
Degree of difficulty: *Easy to moderate, depending on conditions.*
Area's status: *The waters of Jurien Bay form part of a proposed marine park.*

Mike Lapwood

BALER SHELLS

Baler shells are often seen by divers crawling along the sea floor in sandy areas, seagrass clumps or broken reef. Inhabiting sites that range from very shallow to depths of 40 metres, they prey on molluscs such as scallops, tritons and turban shells.

Two species of baler shell live in Western Australia. The northern baler shell is found from Shark Bay to Queensland, whereas the southern baler shell is distributed from the Houtman Abrolhos Islands to South Australia. The southern baler shell has an intricately patterned slug-like foot, and the white lines on its brown body resemble an Aboriginal painting. Both species may attain a length of 45 centimetres or more. Their egg cases are occasionally found attached to rocks or other shells. These large translucent sponge-like cases contain more than 100 developing shells.

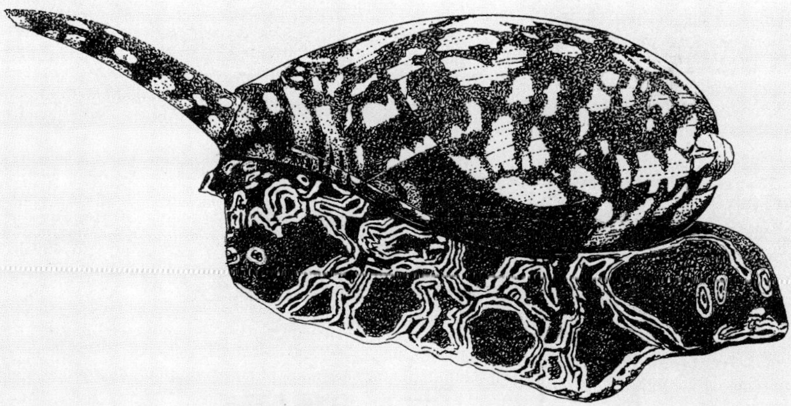

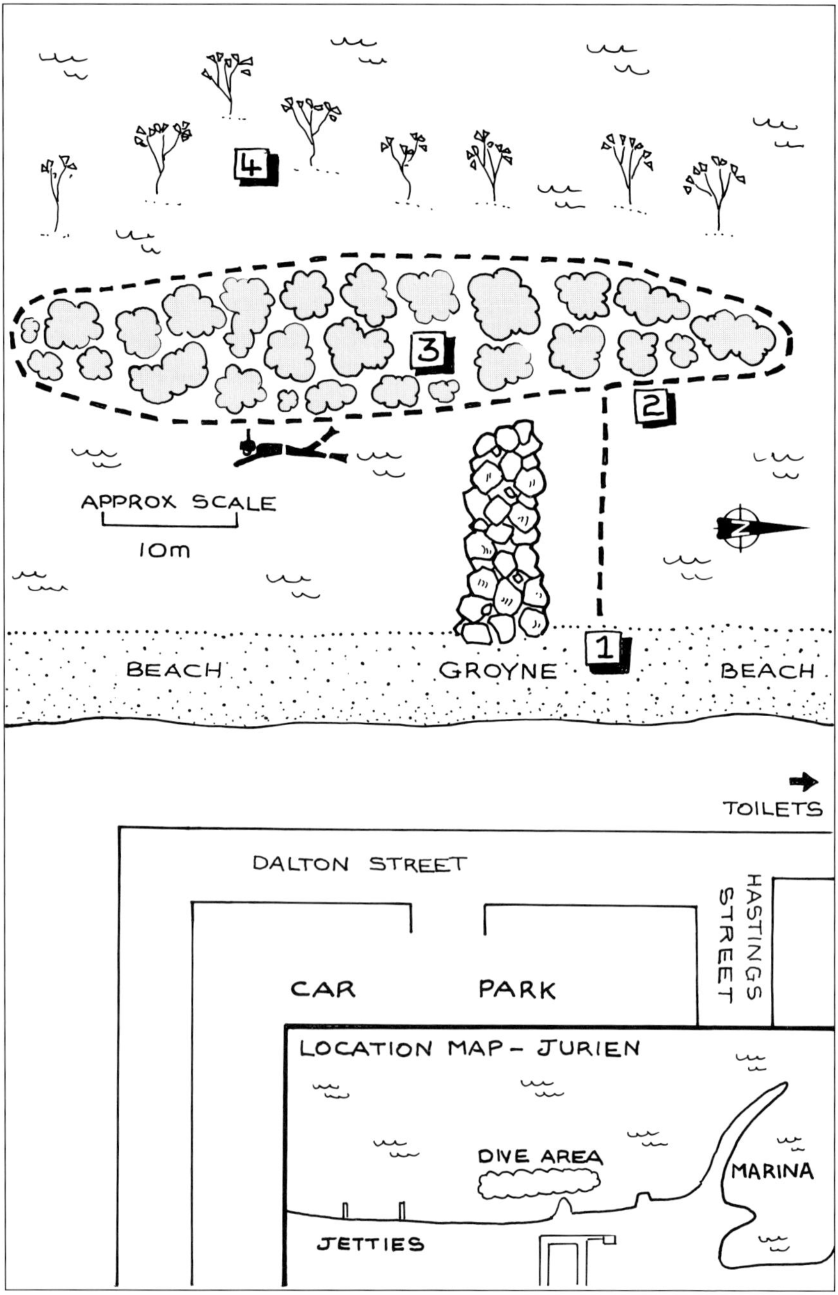
4
3
2
1
APPROX SCALE
10m
BEACH
GROYNE
BEACH
TOILETS
DALTON STREET
HASTINGS STREET
CAR
PARK
LOCATION MAP – JURIEN
DIVE AREA
MARINA
JETTIES

Jurien Town Beach

36

How to get there: *Swim from the Jurien Town Beach.*
Depth: *Maximum of 8 metres.*

At the beach end of Hastings Street is a limestone breakwater constructed as part of the Jurien Boat Harbour in 1983. Here, you can also see the remains of a wooden jetty constructed late last century for the loading of wool and other produce from local farms. Just 20 metres from the sandy beach, the bottom drops off to about eight metres, where various coral bommies can be found. This site is an excellent night dive, with easy access from the car park opposite the beach. Be sure to tow a dive flag at all times, as the marina is only a few hundred metres to the north and boat traffic can be heavy at times.

1. Enter the water on the northern side of the groyne and snorkel out to the west.
2. Follow the slope down and the reef can be found in around eight to nine metres.
3. The coral bombies are in a narrow band running south. The reef only stands about one or two metres from the bottom. It extends from about 150 metres south of the south wall of the marina and peters out about 50 metres from the northernmost jetty. The area is prolific in fish and other invertebrate life, many species of which are semi-tropical and not usually found this far south. Western rock lobsters can also be found here, usually in good numbers, sheltering under the coral ledges.
4. Behind the reef there are extensive meadows of wireweed (*Amphibolis antarctica*). The name wireweed is derived from the wiry stems, which are branched, woody, upright and grow up to two metres long. There are clusters of flat, smooth-edged leaves, with a torn-off appearance, on the end of each branch.

Caution areas: *Beware of boat traffic and always tow a dive flag.*
Degree of difficulty: *Easy to moderate, depending on conditions.*
Area's status: *The waters of Jurien Bay form part of a proposed marine park.*

Mike Lapwood

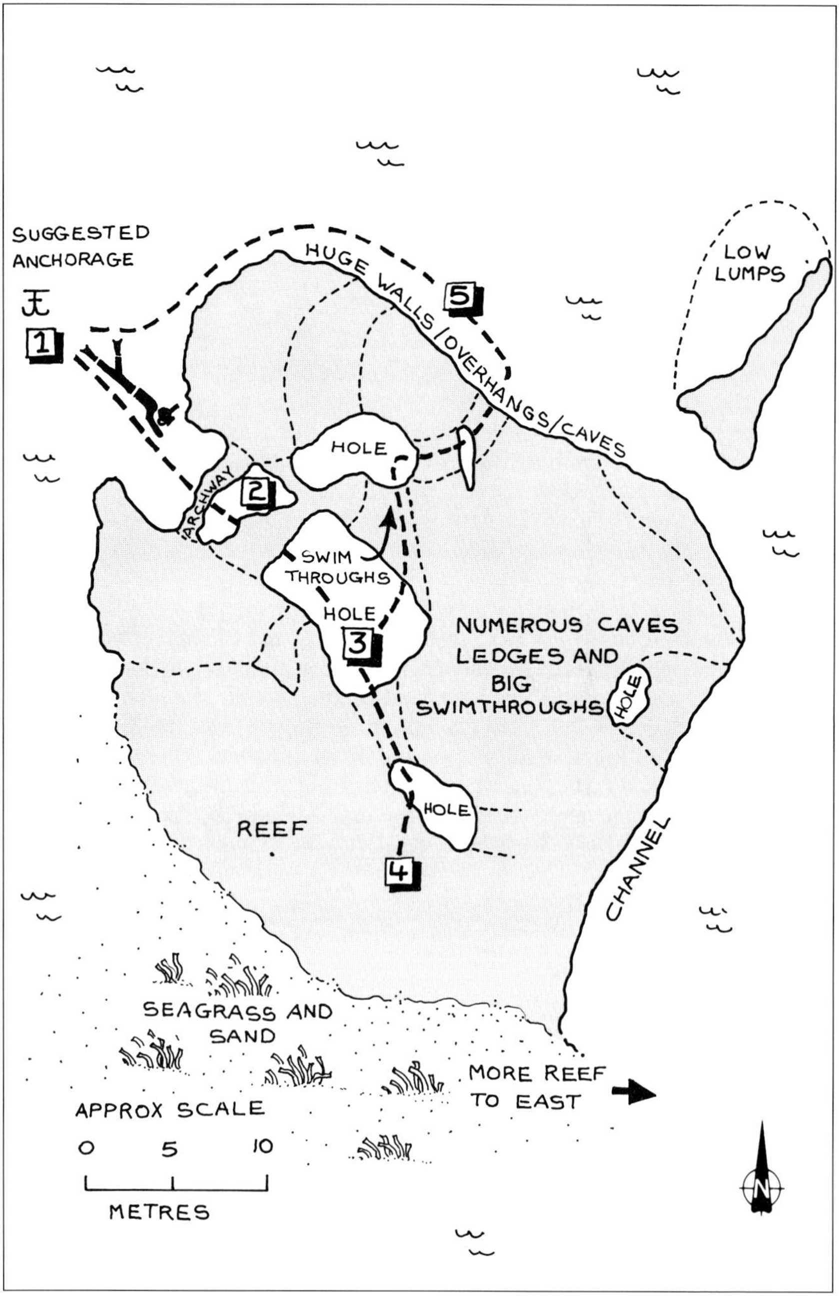
SUGGESTED ANCHORAGE
1
HUGE WALLS/OVERHANGS/CAVES
5
LOW LUMPS
HOLE
ARCHWAY
2
SWIM THROUGHS
HOLE
3
NUMEROUS CAVES LEDGES AND BIG SWIMTHROUGHS
HOLE
HOLE
REEF
4
CHANNEL
SEAGRASS AND SAND
MORE REEF TO EAST
APPROX SCALE
0 5 10
METRES
N

Dogs Hind Leg

37

How to get there: *By boat from the town of Jurien.*
Depth: *10 metres.*

"Dogs Hind Leg" is a unique limestone reef found in the middle of Jurien Bay. The best time to dive it is from February to April, because the area is susceptible to swell that can reduce visibility to near-zero. To get there, proceed out from the marina entrance at a bearing of 320°. When the lighthouse on Escape Island appears over the sandy beach on the eastern side of Favourite Island, you are close. The reef often has craypots on it during the season, making it reasonably easy to find. If an echo sounder is used, the reef appears as a "block", abruptly rising from about 10 metres to within six metres of the surface. Once you are in line with the lighthouse/sandy beach bearing (see diagram below), the reef is 150 metres to the north of the passage (as marked by the passage markers).

The main sections of reef, and the most spectacular, are the western and northern areas, and the total reef is about half a hectare. Huge caves, overhangs festooned with colourful sponges and ascidians, very friendly fish life and more awaits you as you reach the bottom.

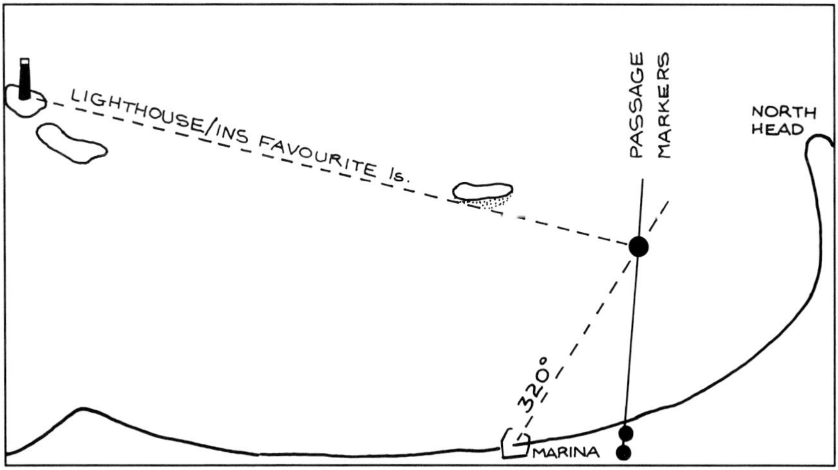

1. Anchor the boat to the west, in the sand, and swim to the north-western corner.
2. This should put you on a large indentation in the reef. One of the reef's residents, a five or six kilogram jewfish, may greet you here or at any point during the dive. This fish doesn't live in any particular hole and is quite friendly and curious. Enjoy the encounter and don't molest the fish in any way, so it will be here on future visits. Swim beneath a huge archway and into the swimthrough behind it and into another huge hole.
3. Here, you are faced with a bewildering array of choices, with about five different swimthroughs to explore, which each lead to different holes or other features. The reef is honeycombed with caves, which are on a number of different levels. As well as being visually spectacular, the reef is so complex that it is virtually impossible to map.
4. To the south, the reef slopes gently down to the seagrass and sand. A large harlequin fish lives in one of the holes about halfway down.
5. To the north, there are huge walls, overhangs and caves, which have some exceptionally colourful sponge and invertebrate life. It is easy to see why this magnificent area is proposed as part of a marine park. It forms part of the longest continuous temperate barrier reef system in Australia, which stretches from Dongara to Trigg. At 300 kilometres in length, it is slightly longer than the 260-kilometre-long Ningaloo Reef. Being in a major zone of biogeographic overlap, it also supports a very interesting and diverse mixture of tropical and temperate marine plants and animals, including stunning corals.

Caution areas: *Remember to anchor your boat well clear of any craypots and always display a dive flag.*
Degree of difficulty: *Moderate to hard, depending on conditions.*
Area's status: *The waters of Jurien Bay form part of a proposed marine park. Please don't take anything except photos.*

Mike Lapwood

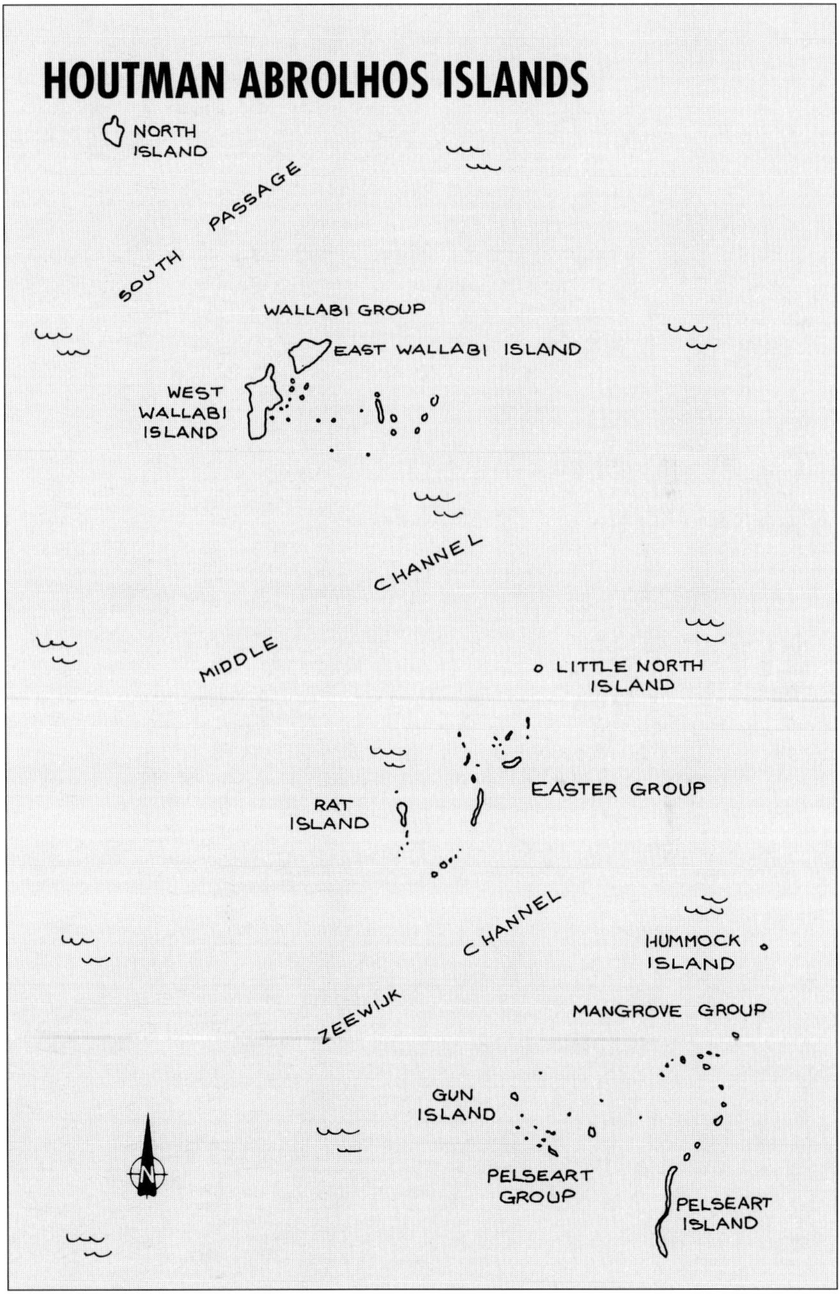
HOUTMAN ABROLHOS ISLANDS
NORTH ISLAND
SOUTH PASSAGE
WALLABI GROUP
EAST WALLABI ISLAND
WEST WALLABI ISLAND
MIDDLE CHANNEL
LITTLE NORTH ISLAND
EASTER GROUP
RAT ISLAND
ZEEWIJK CHANNEL
HUMMOCK ISLAND
MANGROVE GROUP
GUN ISLAND
PELSEART GROUP
PELSEART ISLAND
N

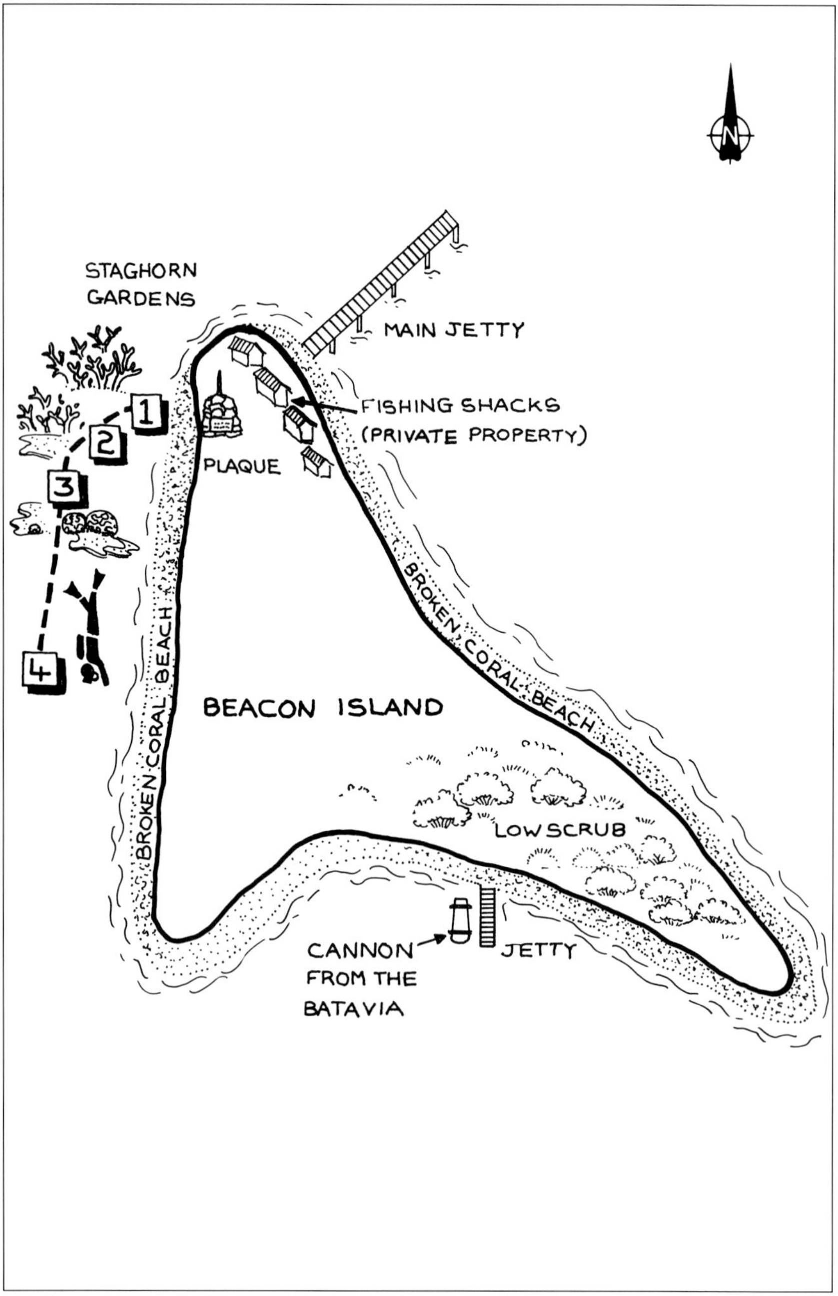
STAGHORN GARDENS
MAIN JETTY
FISHING SHACKS (PRIVATE PROPERTY)
PLAQUE
1
2
3
4
BROKEN CORAL BEACH
BROKEN CORAL BEACH
BEACON ISLAND
LOW SCRUB
CANNON FROM THE BATAVIA
JETTY

Beacon Island

How to get there: *Dive charters are available to the island (contact local dive shops for information). This is the best way to visit these waters, which are highly treacherous, particularly for skippers unfamiliar with them.*
Depth: *Maximum of 30 metres.*

The western side of Beacon Island is probably one of the most remarkable shore dives in Western Australia. It begins in the luxuriant and colourful coral gardens in the shallows and drops away steeply to depths of 20 metres or more. You may even be joined by an Australian sea lion during the dive.

1. Begin your dive on the beach adjacent to the monument to the wreck of the *Batavia*. Some of the most dramatic events in Australia's history unfolded on Beacon Island. Survivors from the *Batavia*, wrecked on June 4, 1629 found their way to Traitors Island and Beacon Island. The captain and 47 senior officers, crew and passengers sailed in an open boat to the mainland to find water and then to the East Indies to get help, leaving 268 people on the two completely waterless islands. A small group of mutineers massacred 125 of the surviving men, women and children and plotted to capture the rescue ship before Pelsaert returned in the yacht *Sardam* three months later. Several ringleaders were tortured and hung in the Abrolhos; two were left on the mainland, others were executed in Batavia (now Jakarta).
2. Green, beige, blue and purple staghorn and plate corals sprawl out to capture light in the shallows and can be seen in only a metre of water. At least 184 species of coral vie for space in the protected islands and along the edges of nutrient-rich channels. Nowhere else in the world do such extensive coral reefs exist so far south. The rich coral communities at the Abrolhos probably owe their existence to the Leeuwin Current. This warm tropical current begins to flow southward at about the same time that corals breed on Western Australian reefs, and hence may carry coral larvae south along the coastline during autumn and winter, and allow them to thrive. In and around the coral live large baldchin groper, jewfish, parrotfish, Moorish idols, raccoon butterflyfish, threadfin butterflyfish and green-finned parrotfish.
3. On the steep drop-offs there are brain corals, giant vase corals and sprawling plate corals. A knobbly-shelled marine snail (*Drupella*), which has caused extensive damage at Ningaloo Reef, can be seen eating some of the corals but has so far not become a problem here. Clark's anemonefish dart in and out of the fronds of the large sea anemones that inhabit the steep walls. Beware of the waving colourful

fronds of an electric sea urchin (which looks like a bizarre plastic lamp from the 1970s), as it can deliver an electric shock if you touch it. You can also see scalyfin, jewfish, moon wrasse, snapper, red-lipped morwong, buffalo bream, angelfish, sergeant majors, long-finned bannerfish and damselfish. A type of nudibranch known as the Spanish dancer may also be encountered. These creatures swim gracefully by undulating their delicate body margins.

4. Explore as much and as far as your inclination and air supply will allow, but always dive within the No Decompression Limits (NDLs) of your dive table and level of qualification, experience and comfort. Unless you are a highly experienced and qualified diver, proceed no deeper than 18 metres. Keep an eye on the depth and your air pressure at all times. Before ascending, ensure that you make a decompression stop of five minutes at five metres. Return through the coral gardens crowding the shallows to the beach.

Caution areas: *The Houtman Abrolhos are the first obstacles in the path of any weather moving in from the west or nor-west. Weather conditions can be highly changeable and cold and warm fronts may reach the islands 24 hours or more in advance of weather bureau forecasts for the mainland.*
Degree of difficulty: *Moderate to hard, depending on conditions.*
Area's status: *The waters around Beacon Island are a designated Reef Observation Area set aside for the conservation and study of resident fish species and their habitats. No fishing is permitted. You are permitted to land on Beacon Island, but you may not use the private facilities (including the jetty) unless you have written permission from the owner.*

Carolyn Thomson-Dans and Peter Dans

SHARK BAY MARINE PARK

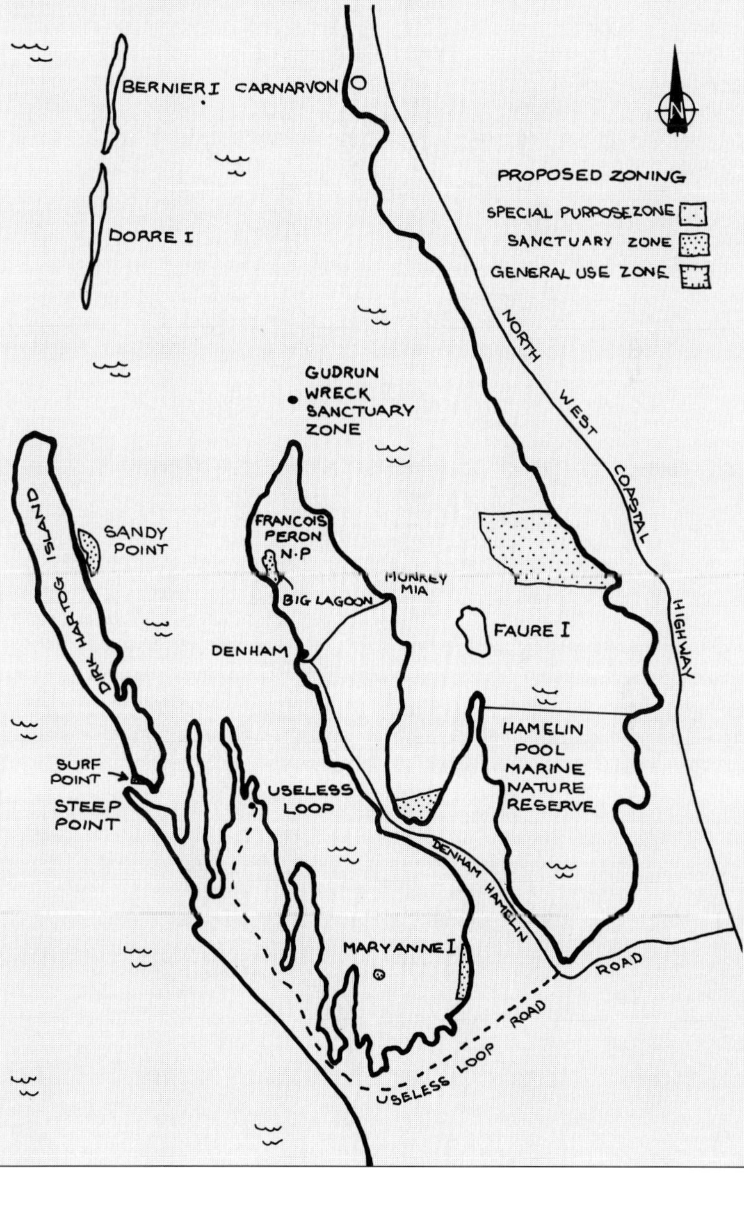

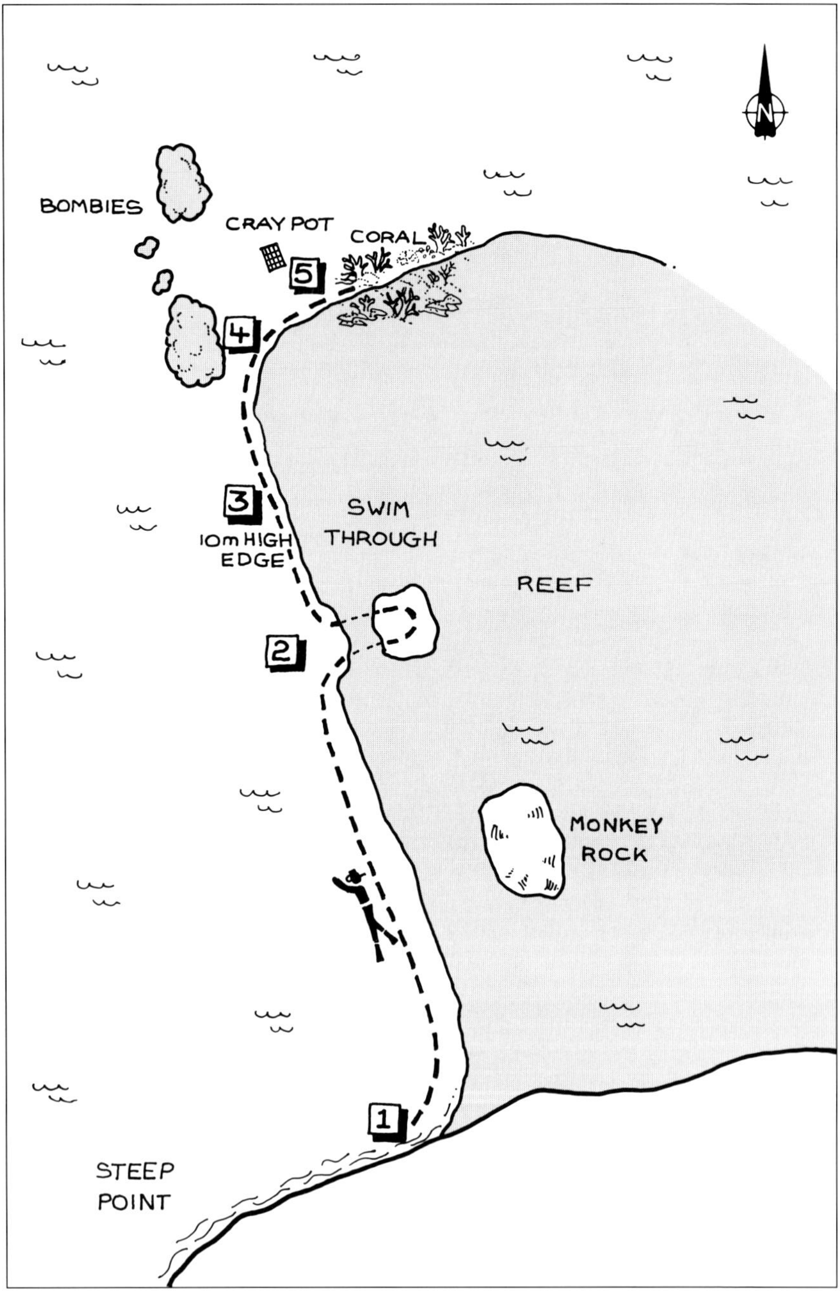
BOMBIES
CRAY POT
CORAL
5
4
3
10m HIGH EDGE
SWIM THROUGH
REEF
2
MONKEY ROCK
1
STEEP POINT
N

Monkey Rock

39

How to get there: *By boat or from the land. Dive charters are available (by request) and this is recommended as the best way to dive the site.*
Depth: *6-18 metres.*

The fault line that runs from Steep Point out and around Monkey Rock is one of Shark Bay's best known dive sites. If you choose not to do a dive charter, Monkey Rock is a 45 km boat trip from Denham and should only be undertaken in a boat at least 5 metres long. If you plan to dive from the shore you will need a four-wheel-drive. Steep Point is a long and rugged drive from Denham via the Useless Loop Road and would involve an overnight stay (camping only). However, do not consider attempting the dive in other than optimum weather conditions. Due to the strong tidal movement in the South Passage, for visibility and safety reasons, the site should only be dived on a slack tide or incoming tide.

1. When entering from the beach, the further east from Monkey Rock the safer.
2. The site has a large swimthrough, starting at six metres and descending to 18 metres. This cavern is full of lionfish and other tropical fish. Lionfish are strikingly attractive but they have venomous spines that can cause painful wounds, so be sure to look but not touch. This area is also the home of two large wobbegong sharks that can be seen lazing in their crevices.
3. To the north is a wall of coral 10 metres high.
4. As the edge of the reef turns to the east, some large coral bombies rise from the bottom. This is the area where large cod and groper are usually seen. Queensland groper can weigh in excess of 300 kilograms and reach more than two and a half metres long. These fish are often curious and may even approach you for a closer look. These large predators lurk in caves and other good hiding spots, ready to ambush tasty animals, such as fish or crustaceans, that venture too near. They are one of our marine wonders and conservation-minded divers will leave them unmolested for others to enjoy. They may live for up to 50 years of age and there are few in any location, so large animals would take many years to be replaced.
5. You then pass an old craypot as you follow the reef edge. The coral along this stage is some of the best at the site. Divers will often encounter mackerel, samson fish, sailfish and manta rays in the area. Manta rays can often weigh more than two tonnes and are able to leap from the water.

The winter months also see a number of whales visiting, so you may be able to see them en route to the site. Between January and April, whale sharks are a common sight in the passage and one may even join you on the dive.

Caution areas: *Dive only on a slack tide, as currents in this area can be very strong.*
Degree of difficulty: *Difficult.*
Area's status: *The waters lie within the Shark Bay Marine Park, which is part of the larger World Heritage Area.*

Brad Barton and Les Fewster, with assistance from Shark Bay Charter Service

MARINE TURTLES

Divers and boaters will often encounter various species of marine turtle. Green turtles are herbivorous, unlike other marine turtles, which are carnivores. In the winter months, baby loggerhead turtles are often carried south from northern breeding areas by means of the Leeuwin Current. The youngsters usually have a shell length between 50 and 80 millimetres and are blown onto beaches between Perth and the South Coast in storms. Loggerhead turtles reside in warm shallow seas and estuaries. However, loggerheads are quite scarce. They mate and nest in tropical and subtropical areas such as Dirk Hartog Island in Shark Bay.

Leatherback turtles have a distinctive ridged shell. One even became entangled in a crab net in Perth's Swan River. Jellyfish are one of the main food items of this species, and this individual would have survived quite well on the brown and white spotted jellyfish that live in the river. Leatherbacks also consume crustaceans and algae. Rather than having the large bony plates which protect the back and undersides of other turtles, they have thick leathery skin strengthened by small embedded bones. They have huge front flippers and are the fastest swimmers of all the marine turtles.

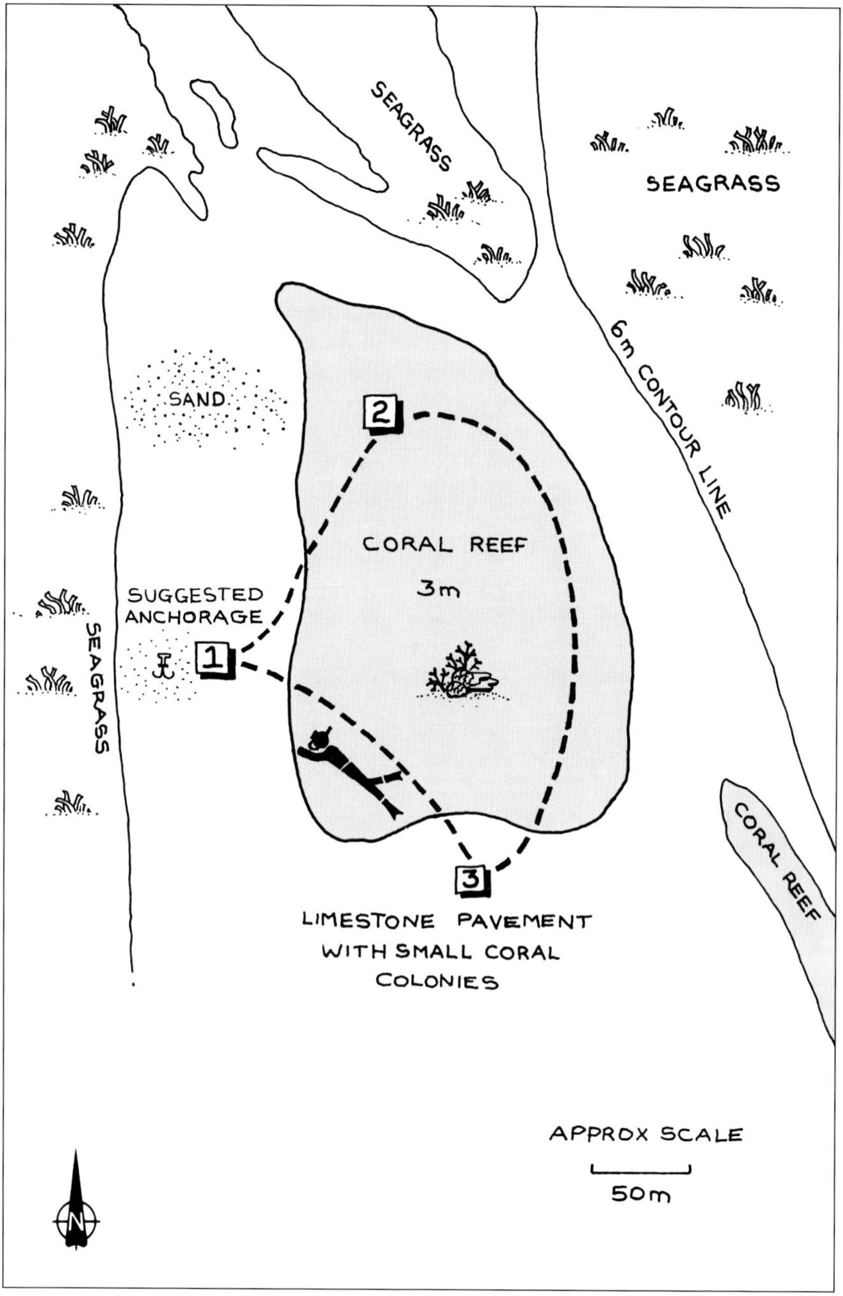
SEAGRASS
SEAGRASS
6m CONTOUR LINE
SAND
2
CORAL REEF
3m
SUGGESTED
ANCHORAGE
1
SEAGRASS
3
LIMESTONE PAVEMENT
WITH SMALL CORAL
COLONIES
CORAL REEF
APPROX SCALE
50m
N

Bar Flats

How to get there: *By boat from Denham. Charters are available (by request).*
Depth: *3 metres.*

Bar Flats is a popular dive and snorkel site for Denham-based boats. It is located at latitude 25° 51.14 south and longitude 113° 20.82 east. It is a coral reef dominated by cabbage corals (*Turbinaria* species). Small fish species are abundant, and, like many other dive sites in Shark Bay, a dugong could be encountered.

1. It is suggested that you anchor in the sandy area on the western side of the main patch of coral. Swim about 50 metres to the coral reef. This interesting area is dominated by cabbage corals, staghorn corals and soft corals. Like reef-building corals, soft corals also have supporting structures of calcium carbonate, but this takes a different form to hard corals. They contain small spicules within their tissue, rather than a continuous skeleton. Other invertebrate marine life is abundant, and includes sponges, sea anemones and yellow tube worms, which live in tubes within corals or other underwater surfaces or animals. Divers do not see the bodies of these worms, just the feather-like feeding tentacles that protrude from their tube. The tentacles trap plankton, which is moved down grooves to the animal's mouth.
2. As you move around the reef, see how many species of fish you can identify. Striped sea perch, scribbled angelfish, butterfish, wrasse species, beaked coralfish, baldchin gropers, bronze bullseyes, sergeant majors and seven-banded wrasse have all been recorded in the area, but there are undoubtedly many more. Blackspot tuskfish, large wrasse which can be recognised by their overall bluish colouring and black spot below the middle of the dorsal fin, live in the areas of sand or weed adjacent to coral reefs.
3. To the south is an area of limestone pavement that has been colonised by small coral colonies.

Caution areas: *Only dive this site on a slack tide. Currents in this area can be quite strong.*
Degree of difficulty: *Easy to moderate, depending on conditions.*
Area's status: *Lies within the Shark Bay Marine Park.*

Brad Barton and Tim Daly

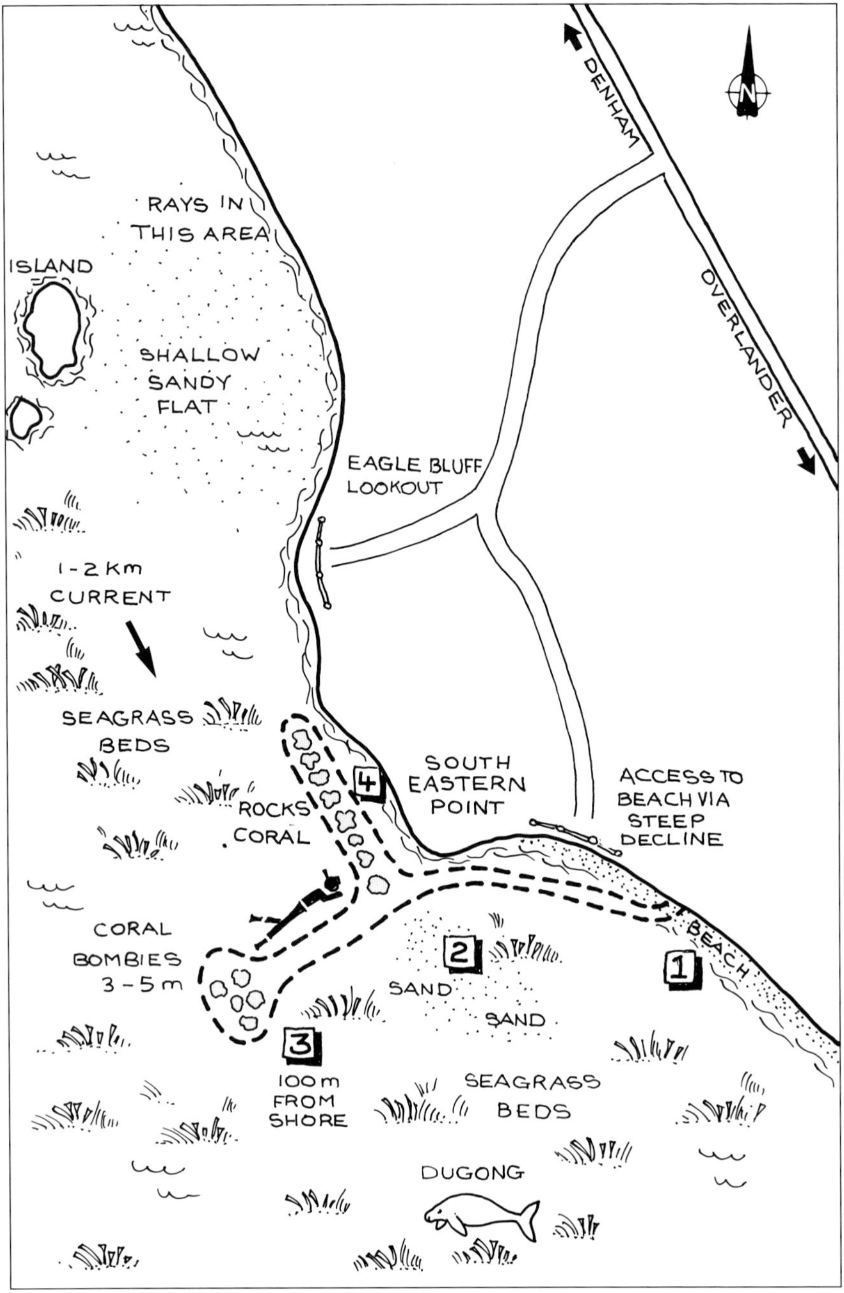
DENHAM
OVERLANDER
RAYS IN THIS AREA
ISLAND
SHALLOW SANDY FLAT
EAGLE BLUFF LOOKOUT
1-2 km CURRENT
SEAGRASS BEDS
SOUTH EASTERN POINT
ACCESS TO BEACH VIA STEEP DECLINE
4
ROCKS CORAL
CORAL BOMBIES 3-5 m
2
1
BEACH
SAND
SAND
3
100 m FROM SHORE
SEAGRASS BEDS
DUGONG

Eagle Bluff

How to get there: *By car (2WD access).*
Depth: *1-5 metres.*

Just 20 minutes drive from the town of Denham, Eagle Bluff is renowned for giving visitors the chance to view marine wildlife from the cliff. Clear, shallow waters around the base of the bluff are ideal for beginners and novice divers to view these marine creatures close up. The site is shallow and perfect for snorkelling.

1. Entry is from the beach on the eastern side of the bluff. The shallow sandy bottom extends 30 metres out, where it meets the seagrass bed. Shovelnose rays and small school sharks cruise along the sand looking for food. Divers entering the water and snorkelling along quietly can often approach them quite closely.
2. The seagrass beds are the driving force behind the diversity of marine life in Shark Bay. Snorkelling over the top of the seagrass, watch for sea snakes, western butterfish and leatherjackets. Rules to obey for sea snakes are the same as their land-based relatives: look but don't touch. Although sea snakes are highly venomous, they are placid and rarely attack people unless provoked and, even when they do, they do not always release venom. Dugongs occasionally forage in the area, so watch for these creatures, which were the source of mythical legends about mermaids.
3. About 100 metres from the south-eastern point is a sand patch with a number of bombies. Small wrasse, blue-lined emperor and tusk fish seek shelter and food around these outcrops. Sea stars, sea cucumbers and sea urchins live amongst the rocks and coral.
4. Swimming back into the area near the base of the bluff, keep an eye out for a variety of stingrays, schools of mullet and whiting, and turtles. The rocks around the bluff shelter small crustaceans and numerous fish species.

Caution areas: *Do not attempt to touch sea snakes and watch out for stonefish amongst the rocks at the base of the bluff.*
Degree of difficulty: *Easy. Ideal for novices and beginners.*
Area's status: *The waters are part of the Shark Bay Marine Park, within the Shark Bay World Heritage Area.*

Certificate of Land Management students from the Central West College of TAFE

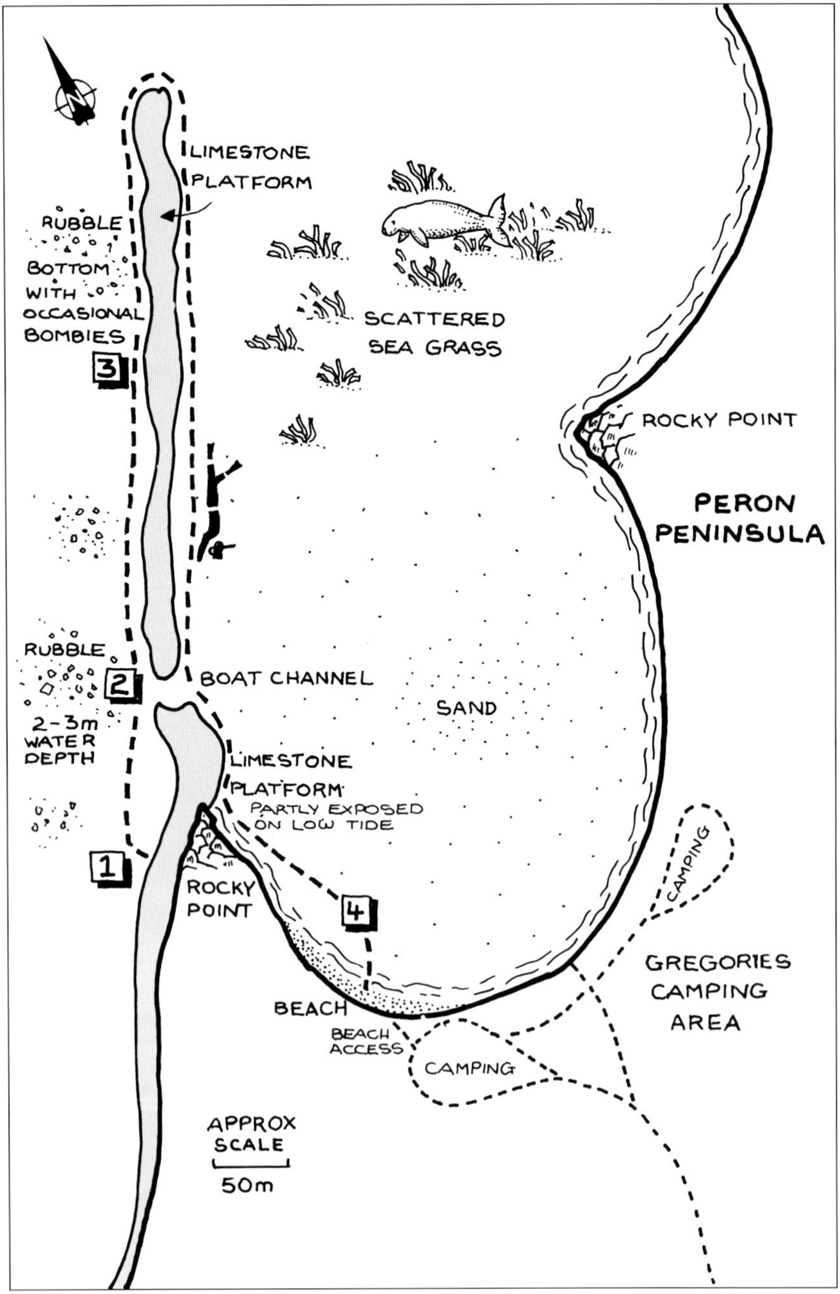
LIMESTONE
PLATFORM
RUBBLE
BOTTOM
WITH
OCCASIONAL
BOMBIES
3
SCATTERED
SEA GRASS
ROCKY POINT
PERON
PENINSULA
RUBBLE
2
BOAT CHANNEL
SAND
2-3m
WATER
DEPTH
LIMESTONE
PLATFORM
PARTLY EXPOSED
ON LOW TIDE
1
ROCKY
POINT
4
CAMPING
GREGORIES
CAMPING
AREA
BEACH
BEACH
ACCESS
CAMPING
APPROX
SCALE
50m

Gregories Reef

42

How to get there: *By 4WD vehicle through Francois Peron National Park to the beach at Gregories camping area.*
Depth: *2-3 metres.*

Gregories Reef is a limestone platform that is accessible to snorkellers from the shore. It supports only small areas of coral and some invertebrates, but abounds in fish life, such as moon wrasse and gold-spotted sweetlips. Schools of mullet swim along the seaward edge of the reef, ever wary of bottlenose dolphins.

1. Walk along the beach to the rocky point and enter the water on the western edge. Take care when crossing the limestone platform, as there are oysters and barnacles that may cut your feet.
2. Swim along the front edge of the limestone platform. Black sponges and fish shelter in the caves and crevices along the reef front, including black-spot tusk fish, which use their tusk-like teeth to bite off coral and pry invertebrates from the reef. The boat channel often has schools of dart and yellowfin bream.
3. It is about 500 metres from the boat channel to the end of the reef platform. At any time snorkellers can cross onto the inside of the reef, as many fish species shelter in the lagoon, feeding on organisms washed off or over the reef. Baldchin gropers often frequent this section of reef. Dugongs are infrequently seen in the scattered seagrass beds inside the lagoon, while dolphins prefer the deeper water outside the reef. Sea urchins often hide in the caves. Take care near them as their spines are very sharp and can pierce even the best diving glove. Sea cucumbers and stingrays can be seen amongst the rubble in front of the reef.
4. After working your way back inside the reef, swim across the lagoon towards the beach. It is easier to exit the water here and less distance to walk to your vehicle or camp. While swimming across the lagoon you may see bar-tailed flatheads, experts in camouflage, or schools of whiting. Many different molluscs and invertebrates burrow into the sands of the lagoon.

Caution areas: *Beware of traffic in the boating channel, and oysters and barnacles on the reef platform.*
Degree of difficulty: *Easy to moderate, depending on conditions.*
Area's status: *The waters lie within the Shark Bay Marine Park. The adjacent land is part of the Francois Peron National Park.*

Brad Barton

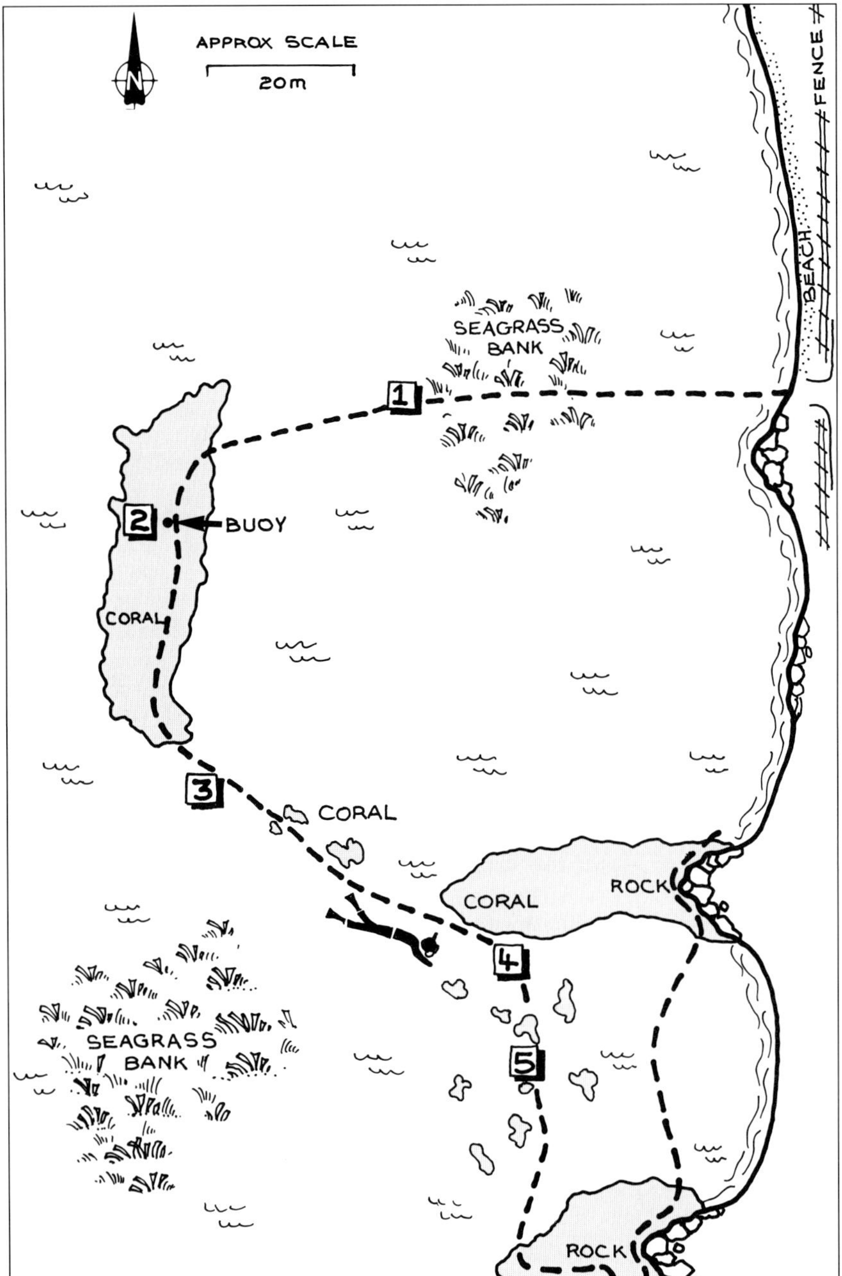
N
APPROX SCALE
20m
FENCE
BEACH
SEAGRASS
BANK
1
2
BUOY
CORAL
3
CORAL
CORAL
ROCK
4
SEAGRASS
BANK
5
ROCK

Bottle Bay

How to get there: *By 4WD vehicle from Denham via Francois Peron National Park. There is beach access from the most northerly campsite at Bottle Bay.*
Depth: *2-4 metres.*

Although quite shallow and not an extensive area of coral, Bottle Bay has a nice patch of colourful corals and sponges, replete with stunning tropical fish. Only 50 to 80 metres off the beach, it is a nice easy shallow dive or snorkel site. Small seagrass banks and areas of sandy bottom, off small rocky points, provide a variety of habitats for a wide range of fish and crustaceans. Turtles and an occasional pod of dolphins can be seen in the area, if you are lucky enough to be there at the right time.

1. Park at the most northern campsite and walk down to the rocky outcrop on the beach. About 80 metres offshore, directly opposite the toilet block, there is a small white marker buoy. This buoy is situated at about the middle of the largest patch of scattered coral.
2. Starting at about 30 metres north and extending about 50 metres south of the buoy is an array of fluorescent green and orange cabbage corals. These are the most dominant forms, but there are also several examples of pale pink brain corals, small plate corals and the very occasional staghorn coral. There are also large, rubbery black sponges to investigate here. This garden is populated throughout by numerous species of bright parrotfish and wrasse, butterflyfish, angelfish and sergeant majors amongst others.
3. Swimming south of this patch, you pass over a large bank of seagrass which can harbour the odd small shark trying to blend into the seagrass as you go by. Heading back inshore at a south-easterly angle from here, you approach two other small rocky outcrops from the beach.
4. About 30 metres offshore, these areas anchor more small coral. Closer in, the rubble, which offers a home to numerous oysters and muscles, is covered by only a metre or two of water at high tide. This area is full of fish feeding, including many small juvenile snapper, butterflyfish, mullet, garfish, parrotfish by the dozen, bullseyes, sweetlip and blue-lined emperor. If a snorkeller is willing to spend time looking under, and lifting rocks, they will be rewarded by the sight of sleepy wobbegongs and timid crabs hiding in nooks and crannies.
5. Look for the occasional anemone and its resident anemonefish amongst the coral and the stirred up silt from a blue-spotted ray or a group of goatfish sifting diligently over the sandy bottom.

Caution areas: *Avoid touching or otherwise damaging delicate coral. Keep an eye out for beach fishermen.*
Degree of difficulty: *Easy.*
Area's status: *Within the Shark Bay Marine Park.*

Colleen Sims and Yvette Pedretti

NINGALOO MARINE PARK

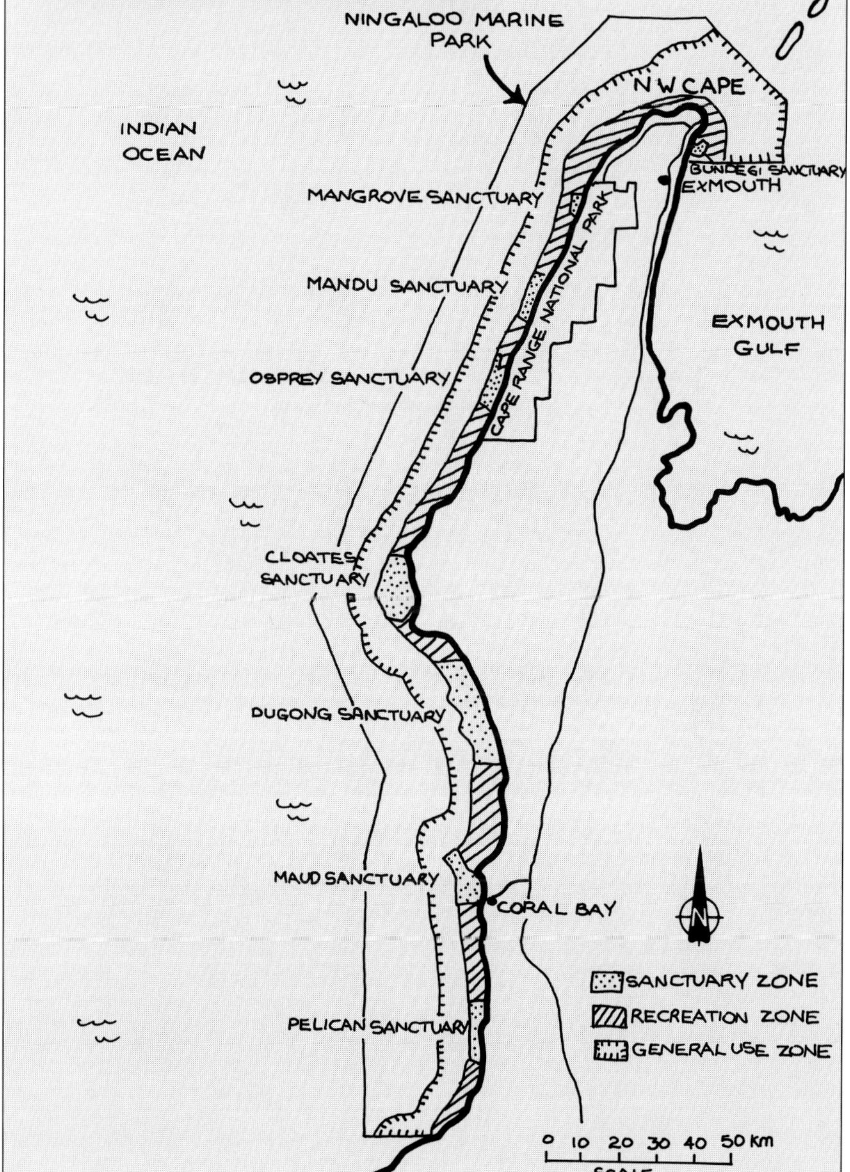

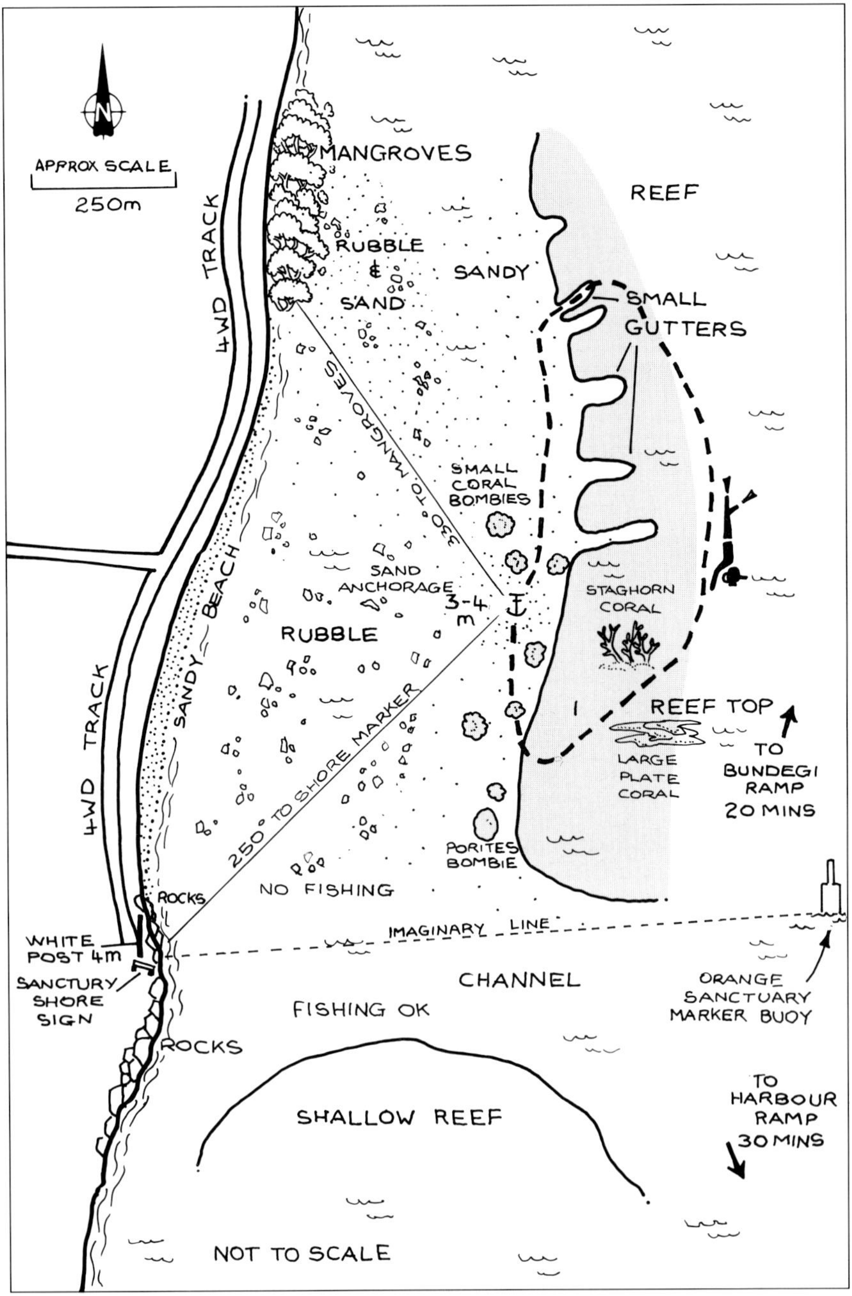

N
APPROX SCALE
250m
4WD TRACK
MANGROVES
REEF
RUBBLE
&
SAND
SANDY
SMALL
GUTTERS
330° TO MANGROVES
SMALL
CORAL
BOMBIES
SANDY BEACH
SAND
ANCHORAGE
3-4
m
STAGHORN
CORAL
RUBBLE
4WD TRACK
REEF TOP
250° TO SHORE MARKER
LARGE
PLATE
CORAL
TO
BUNDEGI
RAMP
20 MINS
PORITES
BOMBIE
NO FISHING
ROCKS
IMAGINARY LINE
WHITE
POST 4m
SANCTURY
SHORE
SIGN
CHANNEL
FISHING OK
ORANGE
SANCTUARY
MARKER BUOY
ROCKS
SHALLOW REEF
TO
HARBOUR
RAMP
30 MINS
NOT TO SCALE

Bundegi Sanctuary

How to get there: *By boat from Exmouth Harbour or the Bundegi boat ramp.*
Depth: *3-4 metres, depending on the tide.*

This is a great site close to Exmouth, especially when it is too windy to snorkel the west coast. The sand/rubble anchorage is easy to find because of the sanctuary zone buoys and shore markers. You will need a small boat with a sand anchor. Either launch at Exmouth Harbour and travel north until you arrive at the sanctuary zone marker or launch at Bundegi boat ramp and travel south on the outside of Bundegi Reef until you arrive at the third (southernmost) sanctuary marker. Visibility varies from good to average, and you need to ensure the anchor holds if the wind picks up. If you don't own a boat you could either hire a dingy or seek the services of a local dive/snorkel operator.

You can snorkel over the top of the reef to view a wide variety of marine life, and it is worth having a look over sandy areas as well for blue-spotted rays, small bombies/cleaner stations, sea cucumbers and turtles. This site does not require a lot of swimming to see lots of small fish – just floating quietly will reveal a myriad of life, including Moorish idols, six-banded angelfish, butterflyfish, coral trout, parrotfish, barramundi cod, sea stars and corals.

As you enter the anchorage, you will pass an isolated coral bombie in four metres of water. This is a large massive coral (*Porites*) with a pretty plate coral growing on the side and a clump of stinging hydroid as well. It is worth a look for all the damselfish (blue pullers) that hang around the top. Remember that this is a sanctuary zone and no collecting or fishing is permitted, but if you want to try fishing then motor south until you are clear of the line between the southern sanctuary shore marker and the southern sanctuary buoy.

Caution areas: *Beware of wind changes.*
Degree of difficulty: *Easy to moderate, depending on your snorkelling ability. There is nowhere to stand up and rest.*
Area's status: *Lies within the Ningaloo Marine Park. Bundegi is a sanctuary zone within the park, in which you can look but not touch.*

Carolyn Williams and Chris Davis

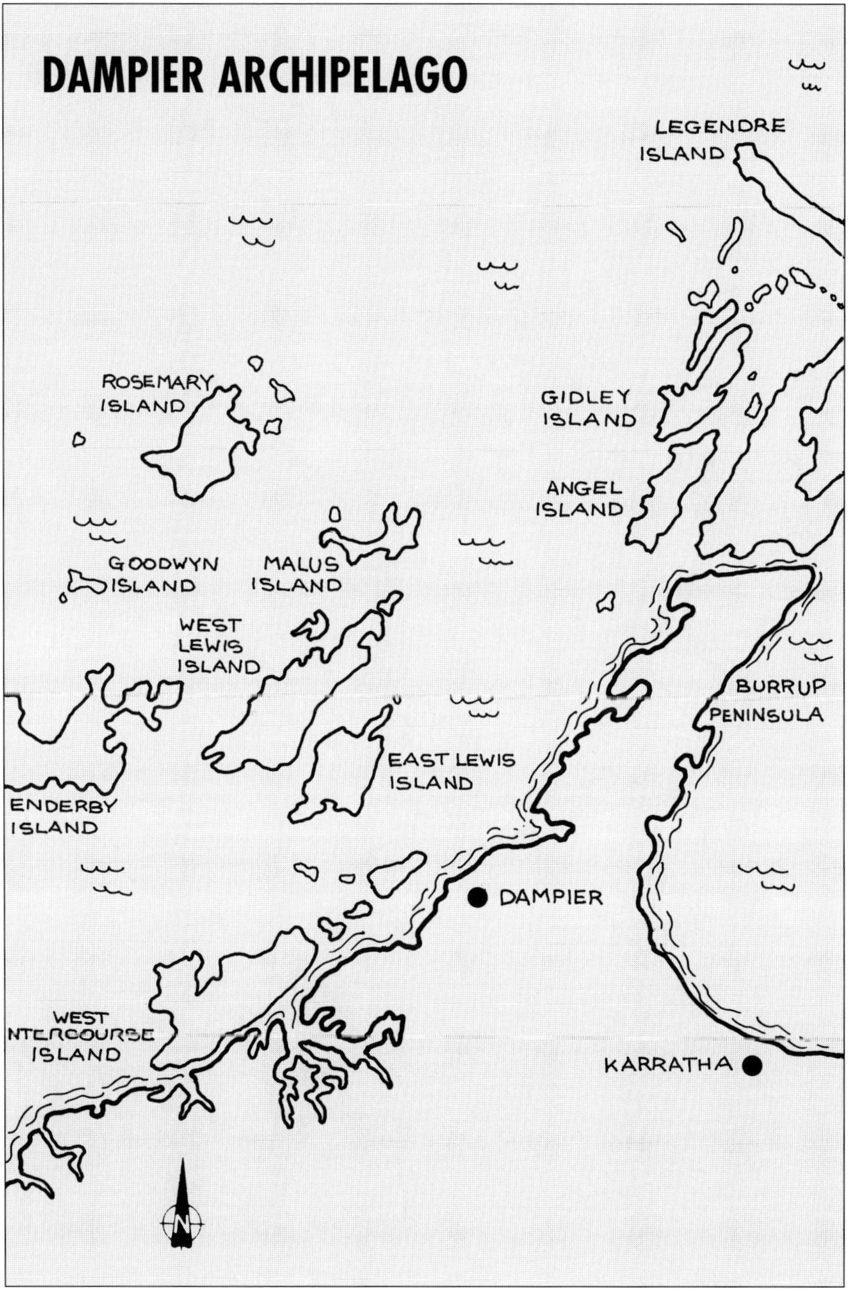
DAMPIER ARCHIPELAGO
LEGENDRE ISLAND
ROSEMARY ISLAND
GIDLEY ISLAND
ANGEL ISLAND
GOODWYN ISLAND
MALUS ISLAND
WEST LEWIS ISLAND
BURRUP PENINSULA
EAST LEWIS ISLAND
ENDERBY ISLAND
DAMPIER
WEST NTERCOURSE ISLAND
KARRATHA
N

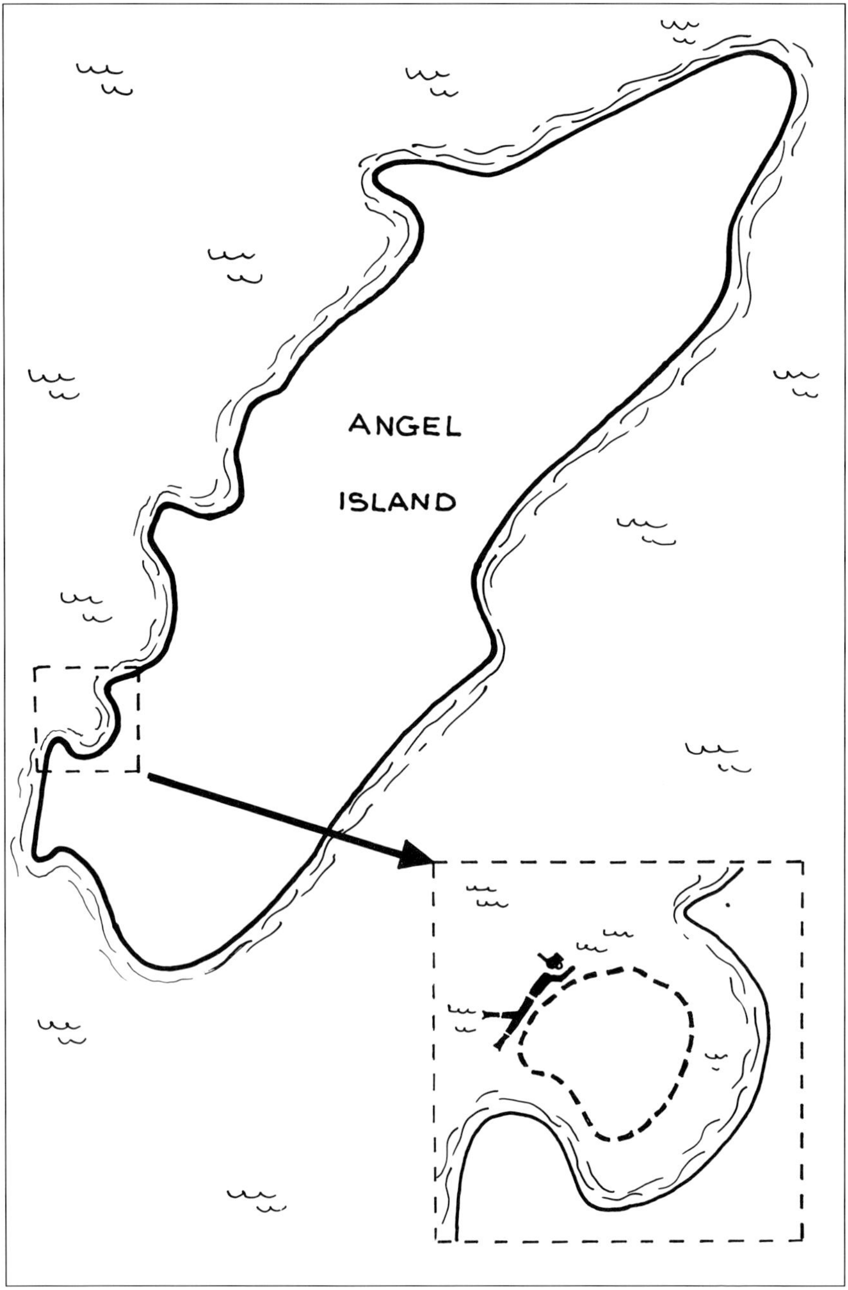
ANGEL
ISLAND

Angel Island

How to get there: *By boat from Dampier.*
Depth: *Maximum depth of 8 metres.*

A coral garden off the south-western corner of the island provides a lovely dive site. The coral area extends almost from the shoreline to a depth of eight metres. This is a very colourful dive, with a variety of coral forms, from large brain corals to small delicate staghorn corals. There is an abundance of fish life at this site, particularly small reef species. Larger fish, such as coral trout and baldchin groper, can also be seen. Look under the bombies to see crayfish, resting turtles and small sharks.

The site can be dived in any direction and no distinct path needs to be taken. Just take the time to enjoy the colourful and diverse marine life that lives here. The diversity of fish and corals in the Dampier Archipelago is comparable to other parts of the Indo-Pacific and many of the species are common to a number of areas. However, peculiarities in the structure of the islands mean that these coral reefs are unique. More than 215 species of coral, many of which occur both inshore and offshore, have been recorded. In inshore waters, corals grow prolifically on rocky slopes, but do not form coral reefs. Most of the coral reefs in the archipelago are fringing reefs and can be found near Delambre, Legendre, Enderby, Kendrew and Rosemary Islands.

The waters of the Dampier Archipelago have been recommended as a marine reserve. Such a reserve would adequately represent the diversity of marine habitats and provide good buffers for the turtle and seabird nesting sites on the islands. It would also contain the most important recreational areas and promote long-term management and preservation. Twenty five of the 42 islands, islets and rocks that make up the Dampier Archipelago are incorporated into reserves for the conservation of wildlife and are managed by the Department of Conservation and Land Management.

Caution areas: *Currents can be quite strong in deeper areas.*
Degree of difficulty: *Easy.*
Area's status: *Angel Island is a nature reserve. The beaches are zoned for recreation including overnight camping. The waters are within a proposed marine reserve.*

Fran Stanley

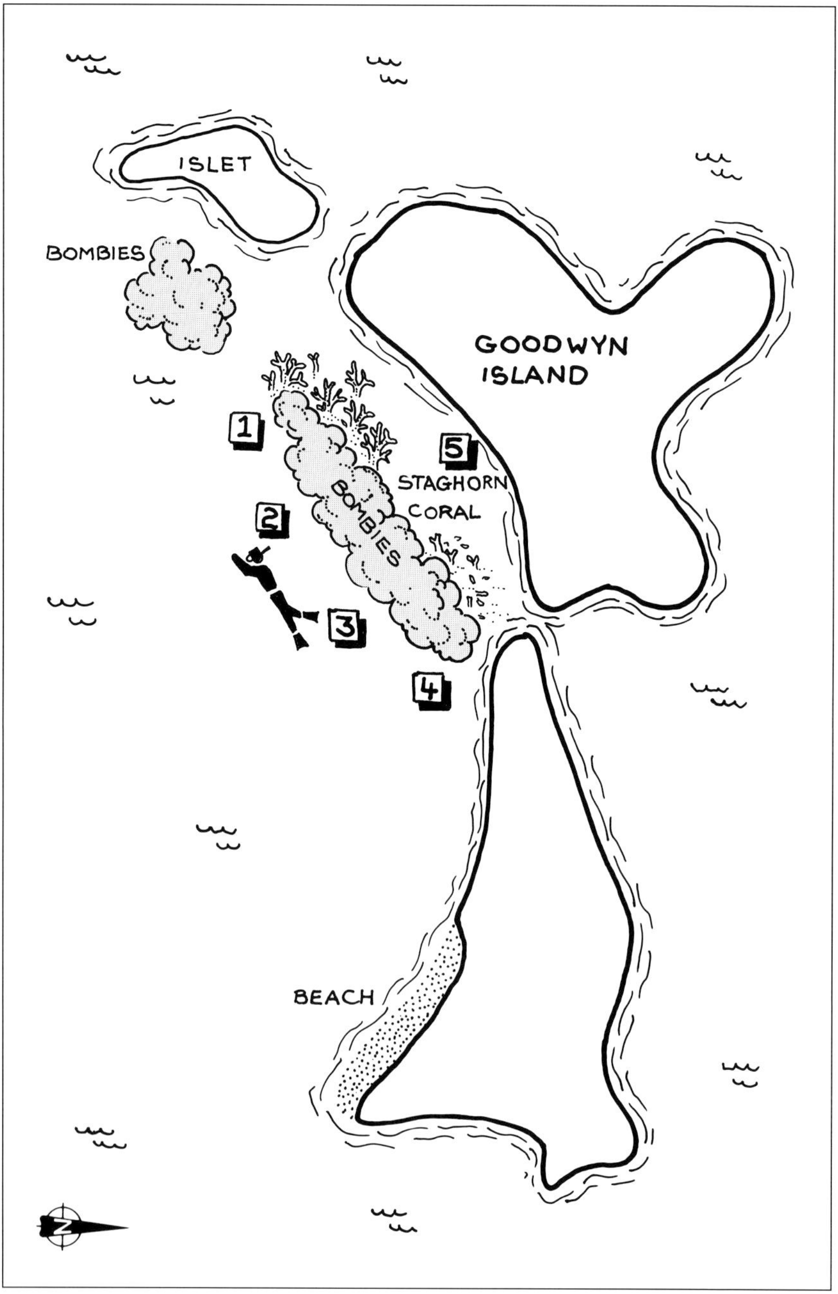
ISLET
BOMBIES
GOODWYN
ISLAND
1
5
STAGHORN
CORAL
BOMBIES
2
3
4
BEACH

Goodwyn Island

46

How to get there: *By boat from Dampier.*
Depth: *1-6 metres.*

Goodwyn Island is actually two small islands. The two are connected at low tide by a sand bar. There is also a small islet to the south-west which has no name. The dive site consists of a line of coral bombies which runs parallel to the southern shore of the island, approximately 150 metres offshore. It starts from the point at which the island breaks at high tide and runs for about 500 metres. A second line of bombies starts about 150 metres south-west of the first and runs towards the small islet. There is a lot of broken staghorn coral on the northern side of the bombies and many small outcrops of staghorn corals at the south-western end of the bombies.

1. Enter the water at one end of the line of bombies. This will depend on which way the water is moving. Then swim along the deeper side of the bombies to the other end.
2. A feature of the dive is the amazing number and range of colours of Christmas worms covering the bombies. The worms come in just about all the colours of the rainbow, ranging from oranges and reds through to blues and white. Some are even striped or multi-coloured. Take some time to watch these small creatures. They will shrink back into their tubes as they sense you approaching. However, if you sit for awhile, you will see them slowly re-extend their fans.
3. There is an abundance of fish life at this site, including schools of many types of damselfish. Spend some time watching these little fish as they dart around in the water. Good sized coral trout and baldchin groper can also be seen.
4. Look under the bombies for painted crayfish, resting turtles and small sharks. Remember that you need a licence to catch crayfish.
5. At high tide, it may be possible to swim on the landward side of the bombies and look at the staghorn corals. Small fish hide amongst these corals.

Caution areas: *There can be quite a strong current at this site and diving should only be done on a slack tide. Wave action can be quite strong across the top of the bombies.*
Degree of difficulty: *Easy to moderate, depending on conditions.*
Area's status: *Goodwyn Island is a nature reserve. Access to most of the island is*

restricted because of the vulnerability of bird nesting sites. However, there is a beach on the south-eastern corner of the island which can be used for recreation. The waters are part of a proposed marine reserve.

Fran Stanley

LIONFISH

The lionfish is a spectacular animal, with brilliant colouring and long defensive spiny fins. It is part of the scorpionfish family, but unlike other members of this family, which often rely on camouflage for protection, it swims freely around coral reefs, leaving its venomous dorsal spines to give it protection.

These brightly-coloured fish, also known as firefish, grow up to 30 centimetres long, and are found predominantly in tropical and subtropical waters. They are nocturnal, becoming active when the sun sets. During the day they are mostly stationary. They show little fear of divers and often orientate their body so that their dorsal fins point forward in a defensive pose. They feed mostly on crustaceans but may consume fish, including juveniles of their own species. They are not aggressive, but take care to stay at least a metre away when observing them, so you are not putting yourself at risk. Show some respect for these beautiful animals and they will leave you alone.

Wounds from the spines of lionfish can result in unbelievable agony. The injured limb should be placed in water as hot as can be tolerated to help alleviate the pain (this breaks down the venom). Medical aid is recommended, as antibiotics may be needed to prevent infection.

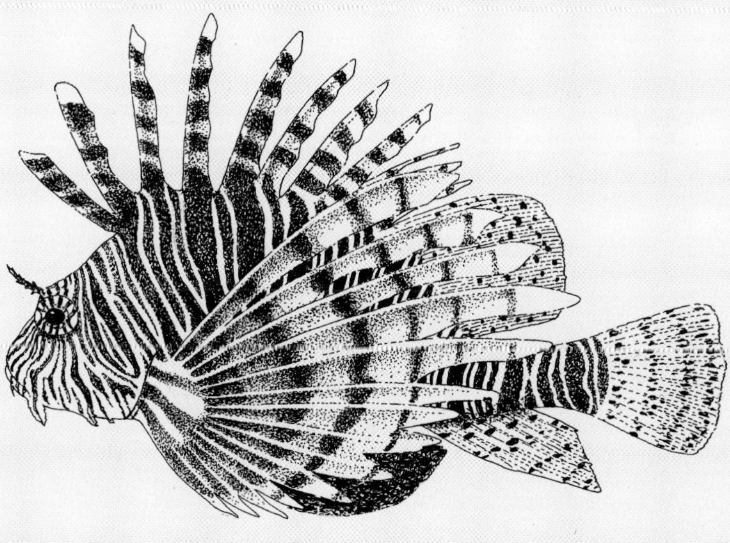

4361 0798 8M